THE BIG BAD GRAMMAR

Slammer!

A DIAGRAMMING GAME

By Karen Newell

Learn For Your Life Publishing

www.kid-friendly-homeschool-curriculum.com

<u>*Dedication*</u>

CARLA
My Sister;
Your Support and Encouragement have been a Delight

ANN
My Friend,
You brought back Sunshine after the long Storm

MARK
My husband,
Your Kindness, Patience, Faith and Humor never wear out

THE BIG BAD GRAMMAR SLAMMER
Table of Contents

Table of Contents

Tutorials

(You may print additional copies of the Clue Cards from the website.

Use plastic page protectors for durability.)

EXPANDED TUTORAIL TOPIC LIST FOR GRAMMAR SLAMMER

THE BIG BAD GRAMMAR SLAMMER
Introduction

"When in the Course of human events, it becomes necessary for one people to dissolve the political bonds which have connected them with another, and to assume among the powers of the earth, the separate and equal station to which the Laws of Nature and of Nature's God entitle them, a decent respect to the opinions of mankind requires that they should declare the causes which impel them to the separation."

Have you ever noticed how eloquent the writings of history can be? Writers were able to produce eloquent sentences that perfectly communicated complex ideas because they had mastered the basics of sentence structure.

And so can you.

Learning grammar is often considered a tedious and unpleasant chore. And diagramming sentences, an art which allows the writer to recognize and control the flow of the sentence, has been rejected by some modern teachers as an exercise too difficult for today's clumsy students.

But this grammar game is intended to take the doldrums out of diagramming, and make you a master craftsman of complex sentences. In addition, it will make you proficient in the use of punctuation rules that go along with well-crafted sentences. This will give you confidence in your writing, and arm you with the right strategies to pass the punctuation questions on standardized tests.

THE BIG BAD GRAMMAR SLAMMER
Overview

There are seven modules in this program. Each module has five or six rules, and there is a short, one page tutorial for each rule.

Here's how you will progress through the rules:

1) Do the tutorial page

2) Develop your own correct sentences which apply that rule.

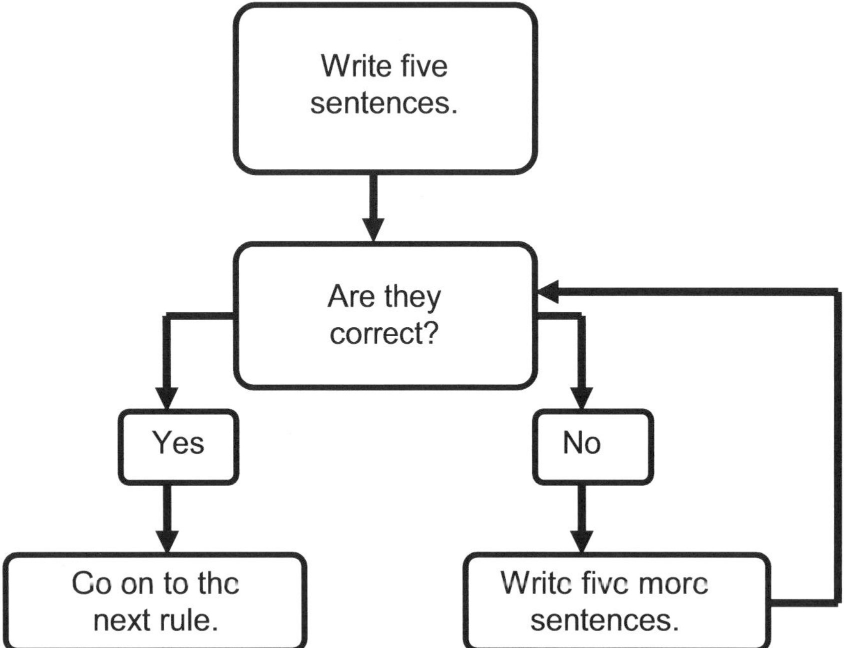

3) When you have correctly written sentences using all the rules in the module, you may go on an optional detective hunt. The detective hunt uses a newspaper, magazine, or other written material you can mark in. See if you can locate examples of the rules in the module just completed.

4) Once a module is completed, you are ready to play the Big Bad Grammar Slammer for that module. You will also include all earlier modules you previously learned in your game.

THE BIG BAD GRAMMAR SLAMMER
Game Plan

In the game you are going to develop sentences using the rules in the modules you have learned. You will try to avoid breaking the rules which will send you into the Slammer while trying to find mistakes to send your opponent there.

For students who do not like competition, the game can be played collaboratively where all participants work together to build a sentence.

Finally, students can also play the game independently without any other players.

Complete instructions for playing the game follow in the next section.

Grading

For grading purposes, these modules can be used to give a student a quiz or a test. The test should not be done until the student has played the game with that module five or more times. More information on how to develop a test appears after the rules of the game.

Review

Review of the suggested order of activities:

1) Complete the tutorial for a rule.
2) When five correct sentences have been developed, go to the next rule.
3) When you have completed all the tutorials for the rules in a module, go on a detective hunt.
4) Then you may play the Big Bad Grammar Slammer Game, either as competition, as a collaborative project, or independently.
5) After playing the game five or more times, a test may be given.

THE BIG BAD GRAMMAR SLAMMER
Rules for the Game of Competition

Needed:
2 or more players
Grammar Slammer Module Cards (A through G)
One dice
One piece of paper and pencil for each player
(Chalkboard or marking board can also be used instead of paper)

1. Before rolling the dice for the first play, each player decides what his or her sentence is going to be about. In the example sentences in the Clue Cards, the player had chosen the subject "dog."

2. The youngest play will go first. The player rolls the dice after declaring what the sentence will be about. The number on the rolled dice will determine what kind of sentence the player needs to write. Clue Card A is consulted to find out what kind of sentence is required. For instance, if a 1 is rolled, a Subject-Verb Sentence will be written. If a two is rolled, a Subject-Verb-Direct Object sentence is written. If the player rolls a "6", the dice is rolled again since there is no 6th sentence on Clue Card A.

3. The player now constructs a sentence using the type of sentence structure assigned from Clue Card A and the subject the player had chosen before the dice was rolled. The player verbally states the sentence and does a diagram on paper.

4. The other players agree or disagree with the first player's sentence. If they disagree a judge needs to determine who is correct: the player who constructed the sentence or the player challenging the sentence.

5. The player who is incorrect (either the sentence constructor or the challenger) gets a point against him. The points can be tallied by each player drawing a stick man, and every time a point is scored against that player, he adds a bar vertically in front of the stick man. He is drawing a jailhouse – the Grammar Slammer. The jail should be drawn so that five bars will lock the stick man in the jail. (This is a non-violent version of the popular game Hang Man.)

6. The player to the right of the first player then declares the subject of his or her sentence, rolls the dice, and constructs the sentence according to the rules above. Other players agree with or disagree with each sentence that is constructed.

7. On the first round, all players construct their sentences from Clue Card A. On the second turn, players will change the subject of their sentences according to the number rolled on their dice and the kind of noun specified by Clue Card B. Instead of changing the subject, a player may instead change any of the nouns he may have in his sentence.

> Sample Game:
> Player A :
> Subject Robin Hood
> Rolls a Two - Subject Verb Direct Object
> Sentence at the end of Round One: *Robin Hood shot his arrow.*
>
> Player B:
> Subject: baseball
> Rolls a Four - Subject - Linking Verb - Predicate Nominative
> Sentence at the end of Round One: *Baseball is a sport.*
>
> Player A - Round Two - Rolls a Three: Personal Pronoun
> Sentence at end of Round Two: *He shot his arrow.*
>
> Player B - Round Two - Rolls a Two: Compound Noun
> Sentence at the end of Round Two: *Baseball and Football are sports.*

8. Some parts of speech may not combine easily with other parts of speech. The new sentence must conform to the last roll of the dice.

9. Players will continue playing until they have constructed sentences for the last Clue Card for which they have completed the corresponding module. If there is no winner by that point, they will go back to the beginning of Clue Card A. When players return to the beginning of Clue Card A, they begin constructing totally new sentences with a totally different subject.

10. The first player to get five bars on his Grammar Slammer Jailhouse loses the game. If there are more than two players, the game can continue until only one player is left.

THE BIG BAD GRAMMAR SLAMMER
Rules for the Game for Collaborative Play

Needed:
Two or more players
Clue Cards A through G
Dice
One paper and pencil for the whole group
(Chalkboard or marking board can also be used instead of paper)

This game is similar to the competitive version, except that only one sentence is going to be constructed. Each player will alter the sentence on his or her turn.

1. The first player declares what the sentence is about before rolling the dice. Then he or she rolls the dice, and constructs that type of sentence. The player verbally states the sentence and then diagrams that sentence.

2. All other players agree or disagree with the construction of the sentence. The group can decide before hand if they wish to give points for correct sentences, or simply to write the sentence collaboratively without any points or winners.

3. The second player will roll the dice. That player will then modify the sentence constructed by the first player according to the type of noun from Clue Card B and their rolled dice.

4. The third player will then go on to Clue Card C and modify the sentence constructed by Player B.

Here is a sample collaborative game:

Player A
Subject: Whales
Rolls a Five for Clue Card A – Subject Linking Verb Adjective
Sentence: *Whales are large.*

Player B:
Rolls a Four for Clue Card B – Infinitive

Player B needs to construct a sentence maintaining as much of Player A's sentence as possible. This is a challenge with infinitives, gerunds, or relative clauses but can be done.
Sentence: *Hunting large whales is dangerous.*

Here Player A challenges.
The judge determines that Player B kept the Subject-Linking Verb-Adjective structure, has an infinitive for a subject, and has maintained the main words of the first sentence.

Player C.
Rolls a 2 for Clue Card C: Prepositional phrase as an adjective
Sentence: *Hunting larges whales in the ocean is dangerous.*

Player A:
Rolls a 3 for Clue Card D: Past Perfect Verb with Progressive Action
Sentence: *Hunting large whales in the ocean had been dangerous.*

Player B
Rolls a 3 for Clue Card E: Adverb modifying an adverb
Since there are no adverbs in the last sentence, Player B must first add an adverb, then add another adverb to modify the first adverb. Player B chose to add "unpredictable" and "quite."
Sentence: *Hunting large whales in the ocean had been quite, unpredictably dangerous.*

According to the instructions at the bottom of Clue Card D, Player B rolled again to see if they would use Card F or Card G. Since an odd number was rolled, the group is going to use Clue Card G.

Player C rolls a 3 for Clue Card G: Complex without a comma
Sentence: Hunting large whales in the ocean had been very, unpredictably dangerous until it was outlawed.

.
Some parts of speech may not combine easily with other parts of speech. The new sentence must conform to the last roll of the dice.

The group can construct as many sentences as they choose beforehand. If points are kept for constructing correct sentences, the winner will be the player with the most points.

THE BIG BAD GRAMMAR SLAMMER
Rules for the Game for Independent Play

Needed for one player:
Clue Cards
One dice
Paper and pencil

1. Before starting, the player states what the sentence will be about. This player decides he will write about model airplanes.

2. Without looking at the Clue Cards, the player rolls the dice seven times and writes each number on a different line on the paper. There should be plenty of room between lines.

The paper looks something like this.

3
6
1
2
2
4
5

Then starting with Clue Card A, the player constructs his first sentence according to the first number written on his paper.

3 Subject - Verb - Indirect Object: *Dad built Steve a model airplane.*

6. Relative Clause: *Whoever loves planes, builds kids model airplanes.*

1. Simple Adjectives: *Whoever loves planes, builds kids realistic model airplanes.*

2. Past Perfect Verb - Simple Action: *Whoever had loved planes, builds kids realistic model airplanes.* (Here, he put the past perfect verb in the clause rather than the main part of the sentence. That is acceptable.)

2 Adverbial Prepositional Phrases: *Whoever had loved planes, builds kids realistic model airplanes in their spare time*

4 Even numbers - go to Clue Card F

5 Appositive: *Whoever had loved planes, builds kids Sky King Models, the most realistic model airplanes ever made, in their spare time.*

Some parts of speech may not combine easily with other parts of speech. The new sentence must conform to the last roll of the dice.

THE BIG BAD GRAMMAR SLAMMER
Quizzing

A simple quiz can be given using the same method described above for independent play. The instructor writes the numbers on the page. The only difference is that there will be only six numbers, and the last number will show whether the student will use Clue Card F or G. For the exact same assignment as written above, the numbers would be listed on the paper as:

3
6
1
2
2
F5

This is because the sixth number is rolled to indicate whether the student should use Clue Card F or G. Since the instructor is determining that, only six numbers are needed.

Once the student has completed all the modules, an instructor may chose to have one or two weekly Grammar Slammer quizzes per week. Even if only one sentence is constructed with each quiz, the repetition will allow for on-going review.

To grade, subtract five points from 100% for each error. Using correct parts of speech and correctly diagramming those parts are counted separately.

Testing

A final test or a quarterly test can be given. The test is done the same way as the quiz, except that the instructor writes the specific sentence parts the students are to use on the paper instead of the numbers. The student is not allowed to use the Clue Cards. For the example above, the instructor would have written:

Subject – Verb – Direct Object
Relative Clause
Simple Adjective
Past Perfect Verb- Simple Action
Adverbial Prepositional Phrase
Appositive

Here, the student needs to know the names of the grammar concepts and not rely on the visual cues of the Clue Cards.

To grade, subtract five points from 100% for each error. Using correct parts of speech and correctly diagramming those parts are counted separately.

THE BIG BAD GRAMMAR SLAMMER

Module A   *The Sentence Skeleton*

Recognizing types of sentences

In this module you will learn about the five different types of sentences.

Did you know that all sentences have two parts?

All sentences have a subject and a predicate.

The subject is what or who the sentence is about. It is always a noun.

The predicate tells what the subject is or did. It always has a verb.

In fact the subject and the verb are the two things you must identify in *every* sentence.

But some sentences might not be complete with just a subject and a verb. The sentence requires more information in order to make sense. So there are four other types of sentences.

There are five different types of sentence skeletons. When you diagram a sentence, the essential parts will be on the main line. All other information will be attached to the line, somewhat like the arms and legs are attached to the trunk of the skeleton.

1. Subject – Verb Sentences

The very simplest sentences have only two words: a subject and an action verb.

Babies cry.

Birds sing.

Ladder fell.

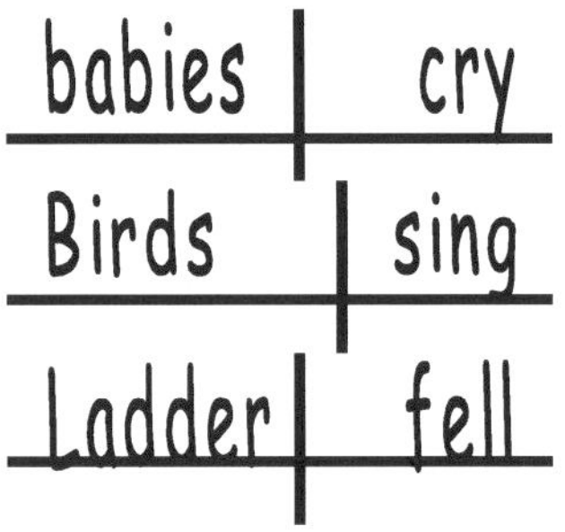

When diagramming a sentence, the main parts of the sentence are written on a horizontal line. A vertical line separates the subject from the verb.

ARTICLES AND POSSESSIVE PRONOUNS
Sometimes a Subject Verb Sentence will include articles or possessive pronouns.

Articles: The words "the," "a," or "an"

Possessive pronouns: words like "my" "his" or "our"
which identify the owner of the noun

Diagram: The baby cried.

Our birds sing.

His ladder fell.

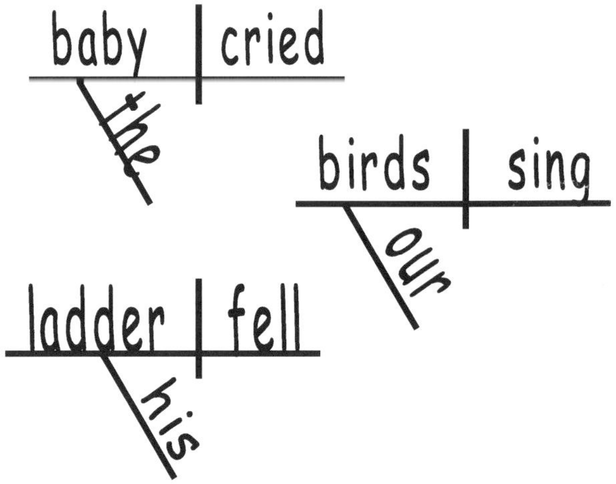

Your Turn: Write five S-V sentences.
You may use articles or possessive pronouns.

2. Subject-Verb-Direct Object

Is this a complete sentence?
  My uncle bought.

It is not a complete sentence because it does not express a complete thought. The reader would think, "Bought what?"

Here is a complete sentence:
  My uncle bought a car.

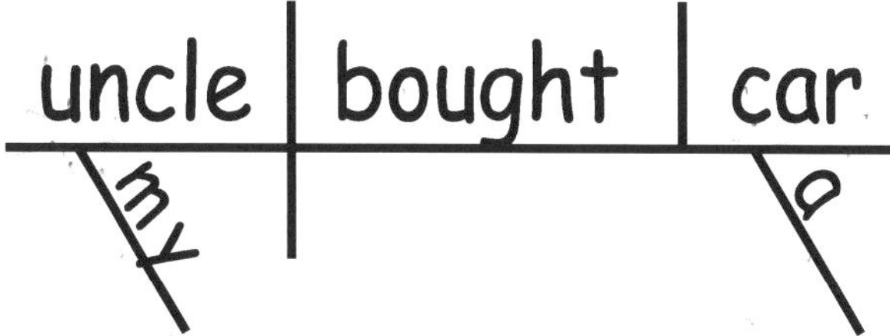

DIRECT OBJECT
A direct object is a noun that receives the action of the verb.

Here is a clue to indicate the presence of a direct object:

Say the subject, then the action verb, then ask "what?"

Diagramming
To diagram an S-V-DO sentence, a vertical line that does not cross the main line is made separating the action verb from the direct object.

Diagram the following sentences (use the example above as a model)

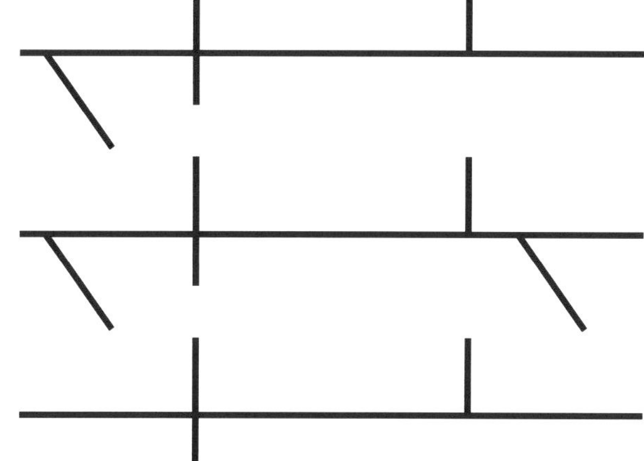

Our neighbor cooks steak.

The children hid their toys.

Birds eat worms.

Your turn: Write your own 5 S-V-DO sentences and diagram them.

3. Subject--Action Verb--Indirect Object--Direct Object

There is another type of sentence, very similar to S-V-DO, and it is really not all that common to find. However, when students do read or write a sentence with an indirect object, it often confuses them if they aren't familiar with it.

My mother bought my sister a new dress.

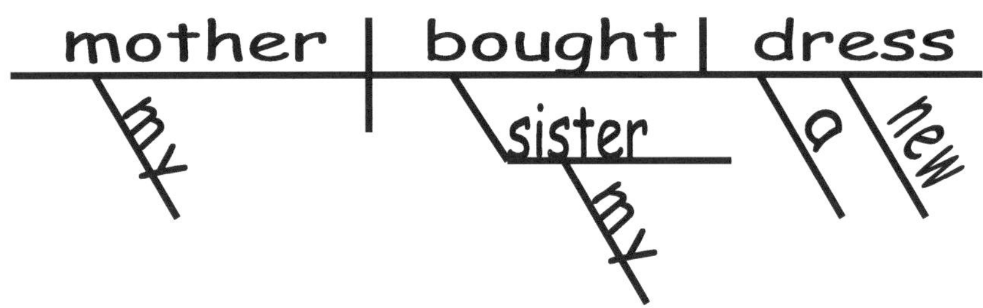

The subject-verb is "Mother bought." What did mother buy: the sister or the dress?

Of course she bought the dress. In this case the sister is the indirect object.

INDIRECT OBJECT
A noun which the action of the verb is directed to is the indirect object.

Jan found Tony an umbrella.

Grandma sewed Kara a dress.

Timothy brought Uncle Alex coffee.

Notice that in most of these sentences, the verb indicates the subject "gave" something to the indirect object.

Here are two clues to help you identify an indirect object.

1. Say the subject, then the verb, then ask, "What?" The direct object answers the question "What?" If another noun is between the verb and the direct object, it is an indirect object.

For example:
> ***Timothy bought Uncle Alex coffee.***
> Timothy bought what? Coffee.
> The direct object is coffee.
> Uncle Alex is an indirect object between the verb "brought"
> > and the direct object "coffee."

2. If the verb is a synonym for give, put the word "to" or "for" in front of the noun. If the sentence means the same thing, it is an indirect object.

For example:
> ***Timothy brought Uncle Alex coffee.***
> > means the same thing as,
> ***Timothy brought for Uncle Alex coffee.***
> Uncle Alex is an indirect object.

DIAGRAMMING
The indirect object will not stay on the main line. In reality, we treat it as a prepositional phrase (which you will learn about later) because we understand that the object was given to that person.

Your Turn:
> Create and diagram five S-AV-IO-DO sentences.

4. Subject – Linking Verb –Predicate Nominative
S-LV-PN

This girl is my neighbor.

Can you find an action verb in that sentence?
There isn't one. Now is a good time to introduce you to the other type of verb.

LINKING VERBS

Linking verbs are the "to be" verbs which connect the subject to the predicate and indicate the person and the tense of the verb

Well that was certainly clear wasn't it? Actually, you have been correctly using this concept since you were three years old.

SINGULAR
     1st Person   I **am** the neighbor.
     2nd Person   You **are** the neighbor.
     3rd Person   He **is** the neighbor. (Or she is the neighbor)

PLURAL
     1st Person   We **are** the neighbors.
     2nd Person   You **are** the neighbors.
     3rd Person   They **are** the neighbors.

The linking verbs changed according to whether the subject was first, second, or third person. It will also change if the verb is in the past tense. Then it would be:

                 I **was** the neighbor.
                 You **were** the neighbor. etc.

PREDICATE NOMINATIVE

The noun in the predicate that expresses the state of the subject is the predicate nominative.

Remember, there are two main parts of the sentence; the subject is on one side of the vertical line and the predicate is on the other.

Nominative is another word for the subject, so this phrase seems like a contradiction. What it means is:

a noun that renames the subject.

Clue: You can tell you have a Predicate Nominative if you can switch the subject and the noun in the predicate and the sentence still makes sense.

Larry is my friend.	My friend is Larry.
Mrs. Smith was our teacher.	Our teacher was Mrs. Smith
This cake is my dessert.	My dessert is this cake.

Notice in these sentences that the subject and the predicate nominative are the same.

Larry = friend
Mrs. Smith = teacher
cake = dessert

DIAGRAMMING
This is similar to the diagram for the direct object, but you will notice that the line is at a slant.

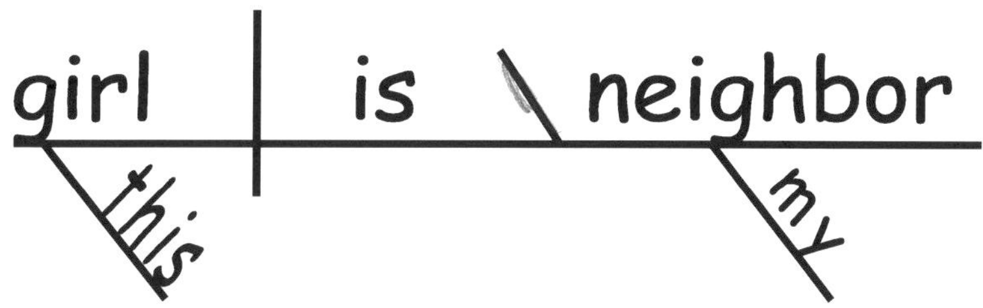

Here is a reminder to help you remember which direction to slant the line when you have a direct object. Direct Objects are always nouns, so remember "N" for noun.

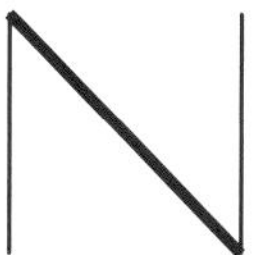

5. Subject – Linking Verb –Adjective
S-LV-Adj

Compare these two sentences:

S-LV-PN **This girl is my neighbor.**
S-LV-Adj **This girl is friendly.**

The top sentence has a Predicate Nominative, which is a noun that restates the subject. The bottom sentence has an adjective, a word that describes the subject.

CLUE:

If it is a Predicate Nominative, the word that answers "What?" to the verb is a noun. It is the same person or thing as the noun in the subject. (girl and neighbor are the same person)

If it is a Predicate Adjective, the word that answers "What?" to the verb is an adjective. It describes the subject.

ANOTHER CLUE:

You could put the adjective in the predicate in front of the subject and it would make sense.

For example: friendly girl

Notice you can put the Predicate Adjective in front of each subject in the S-LV-Adj. sentences below.

Chili is spicy.

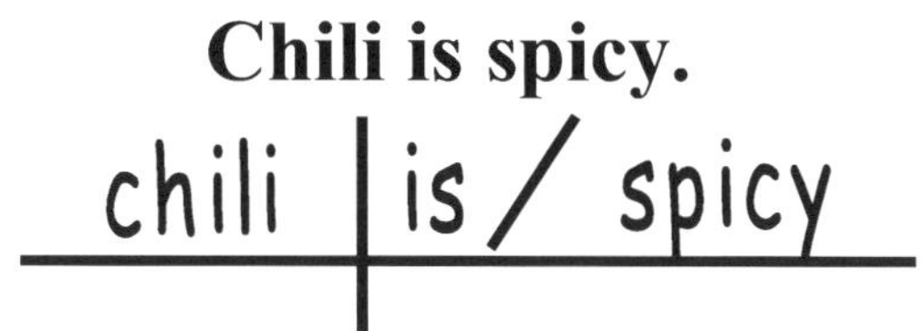

The night will be cold.

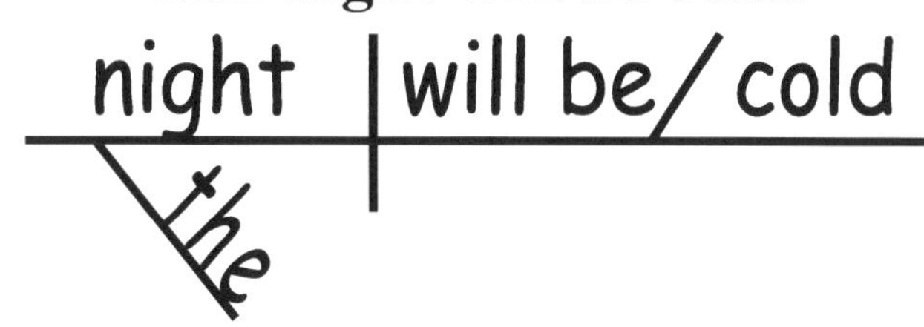

DIAGRAMMING

The diagramming frame for S-LV-Adj sentences is similar to the frames you have used before. The difference is the direction of the slant between the verb and the adjective.

 Here is a clue to help you remember the slant of the line with a predicate adjective:

Try diagramming these Subject-Linking Verb-Adjective Sentences:

Timothy was tired.

My muscles have been sore.

Their kitten was furry.

Now that you have completed all of Module A, you might want to go on a detective hunt for Sentence Skeletons. All sentences will have one of these types of sentence skeletons. Use a newspaper or other written material you can mark up. Put the letters S, V, LV, DO, IO, PN and Adj over the correct words.

Now, you are ready to play the first round of The Big Bad Grammar Slammer. See the directions at the beginning of the book to find the rules of the game.

THE BIG BAD GRAMMAR SLAMMER
Module B   *Nouns*

A noun is a person, place, thing, or idea.

Clue:

The words "the" or "a" or "my" can go in front of a noun. Whenever you see those words, it signals that a noun will follow.

The subject of the sentence is always a noun.

Whether you are writing a sentence or analyzing one that has been written, the first thing to do is to identify the subject.

In this module, you will learn different types of nouns. Some of them can be a little bit tricky. In most cases, you will develop a sentence with a particular noun type as the subject.

As we learned before, nouns can also be the direct object, the indirect object, or the predicate nominative.

EXCHANGE

A subject is a noun. In this module, when you are asked to write a specific type of noun for subject, you can make an exchange. In that case, instead of using that kind of noun for the subject, you can use if for the direct object, indirect object, or predicate nominative, if you choose.

1. Proper Nouns

A proper noun gives the name of a specific place or person.

COMMON NOUN	PROPER NOUN
street	Main Street
dog	Rover
actor	John Wayne
park	River Valley Park
mountain	Mt. Rushmore
holiday	Christmas Day
relative	Uncle John
president	President Hoover

PUNCTUATION PEST
(A pesky rule to remember)
The *entire* proper noun phrase is capitalized.
<u>T</u>hanksgiving <u>D</u>ay
<u>B</u>radstone <u>R</u>iver

DIAGRAMMING

There is no change in the diagramming frame for proper nouns. In this program, the entire name will be placed on the main line.

2. Compound Nouns

A compound noun exists when two or more nouns share the position of subject, direct object, or predicate nominative.

SUBJECT
The boy and girl are talking.

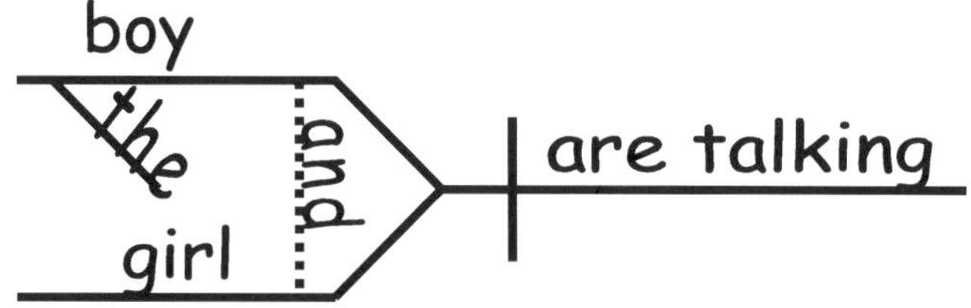

Lisa or Tom will come.

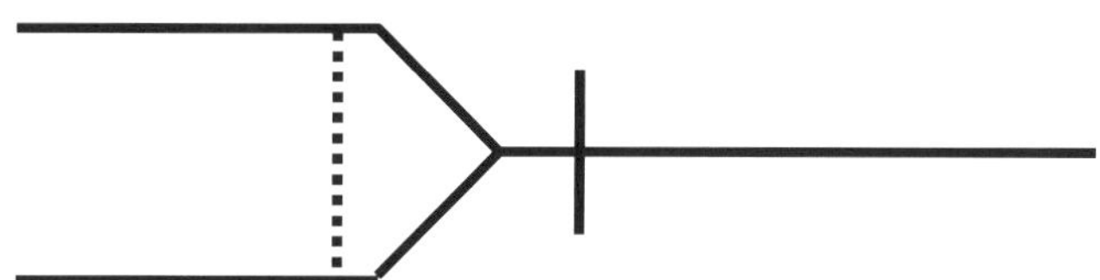

DIRECT OBJECT
She made brownies and cupcakes.

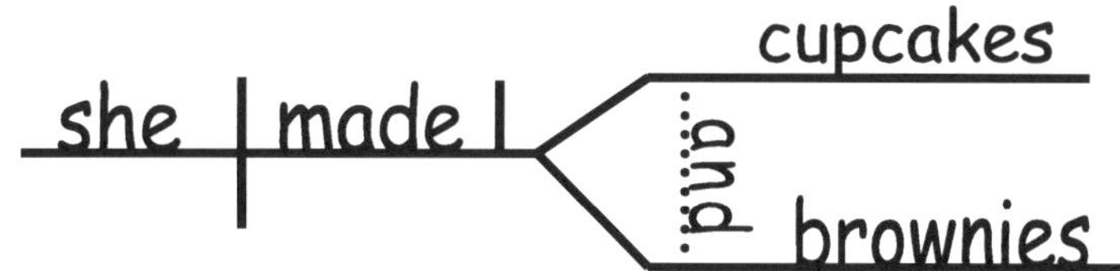

Our garden produced carrots and peas.

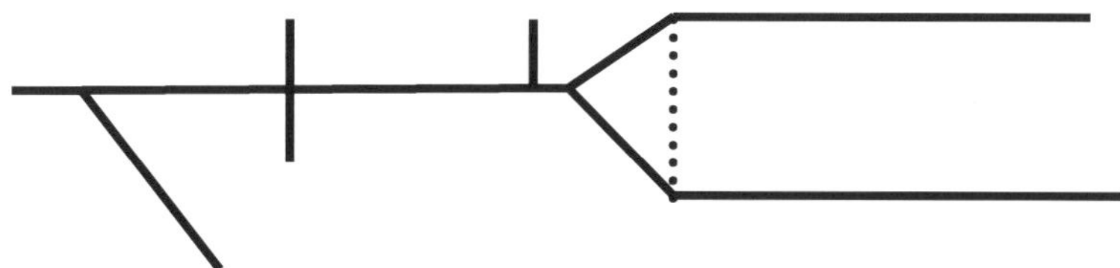

PREDICATE NOMINATIVE

I am a football player and soccer player.

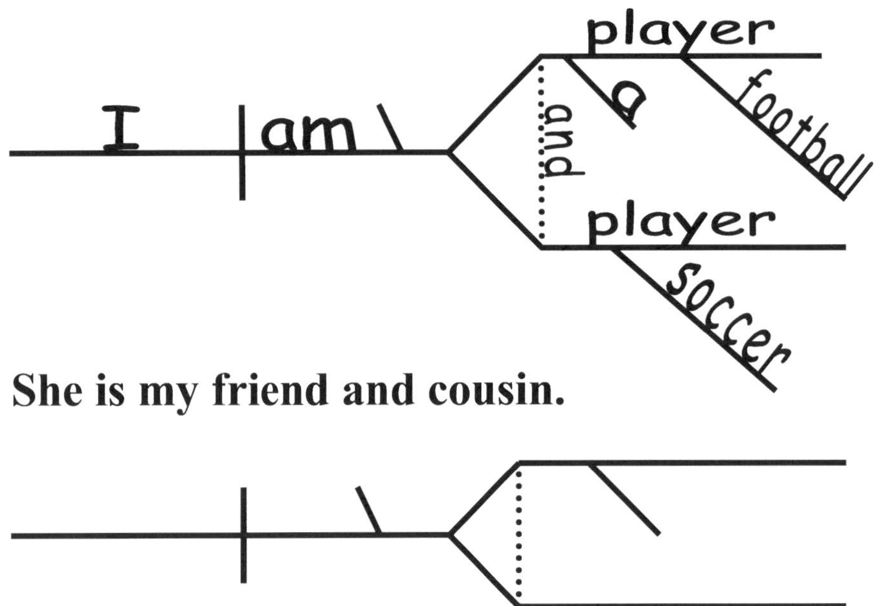

She is my friend and cousin.

3. Personal Pronouns

A personal pronoun replaces a noun.

PERSON		NOMINATIVE CASE	OBJECTIVE CASE
S I N G U L A R	1st 2nd 3rd	I You He, She, It	Me You Him, Her, It
P L U R A L	1st 2nd 3rd	We You They	Us You Them

CLUE

To find the ***nominative case***, use this sentence as a sample:

_____________ found it.

Example: I found it. She found it. They found it. etc.

To find the ***objective case***, use this sentence as a sample:

He found _____________.

Example: He found me. He found them. He found you. etc.

ANTECEDENT

An antecedent is the noun the personal pronoun is replacing.

In order for the sentence to communicate and make sense, it is necessary to know the antecedent.

"He found it." Doesn't make any sense unless you know what the "he" and "it" are referring to.

"Larry was looking for his watch. He found it in the garage."

Now it makes sense. The antecedent for "he" is "Larry." The antecedent for "it" is watch.

DIAGRAMMING
The diagram frame does not change when a personal pronoun is used.

He is sleeping.

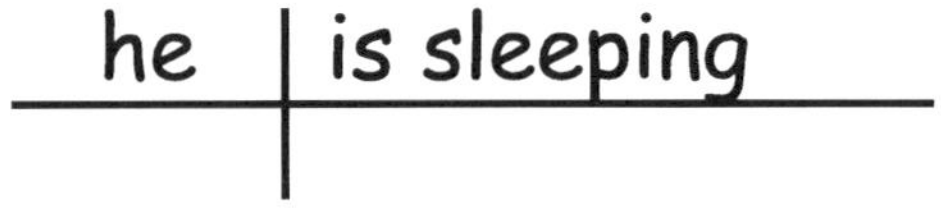

<u>   he | is sleeping   </u>

YOUR TURN:
Replace some nouns with personal pronouns in a book you have read.

4. Infinitive

An infinitive is the word "to" with a verb, and it takes the place of a noun.

Read that again, and see if it made any sense.

Maybe these examples will make sense. Notice the bolded section looks like a verb, but functions like a noun.

SUBJECT

To sleep is a luxury.   N LV PN

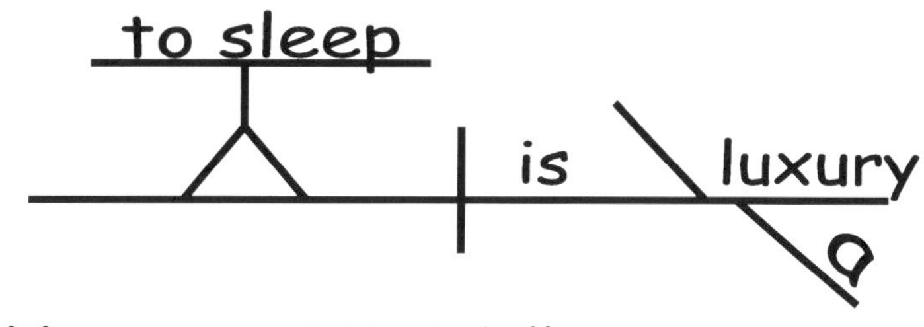

To fly is exciting.   N LV Adj

DIRECT OBJECT

I like **to study**.   N LV DO

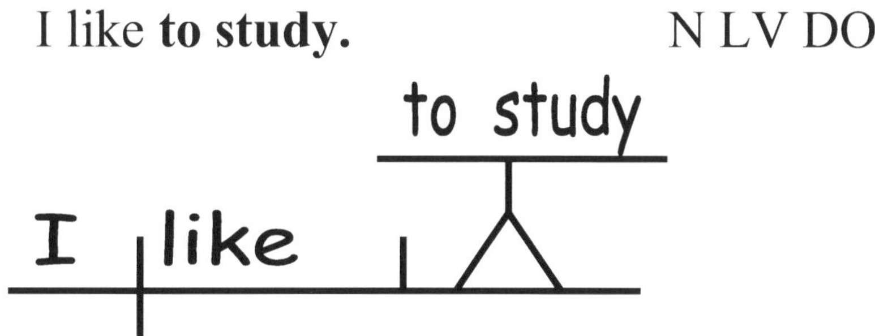

He likes **to play.**   N LV DO

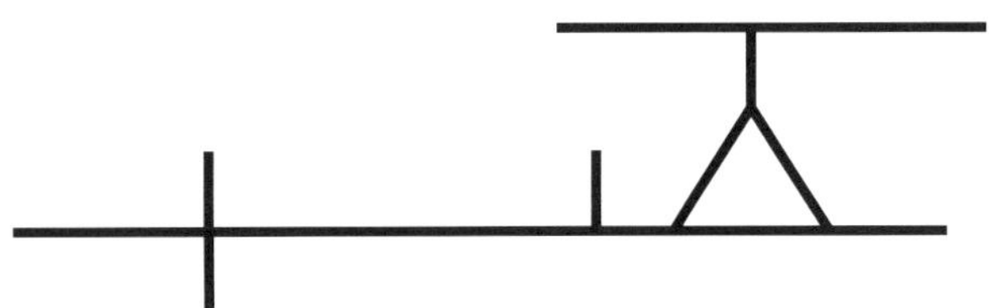

DIAGRAMMING

Infinitives are diagrammed with a stick figure lifting them off the frame.

CLUE
To + Verb

5. Gerund

A gerund is a verb form that is used as a noun.
Compare these sentences:

1.   That book is my favorite.
2.   Skiing is my favorite.

In the first sentence, do you agree that "book" is the subject of the sentence and is a noun? In the second sentence, skiing is used the same way that book is, but we usually think of skiing as a verb. In this case it is a gerund--a verb which is used as a noun.

Sometimes the verb used as a gerund has a direct object, but the gerund is still the subject.

DIAGRAMMING
The gerund is diagrammed on a curved line. Any direct object that takes the action of the gerund will be placed on the other side of a vertical divider. If the gerund is the subject of the sentence, it is lifted off the main frame by a stick figure.

Shooting basketballs is my favorite game.

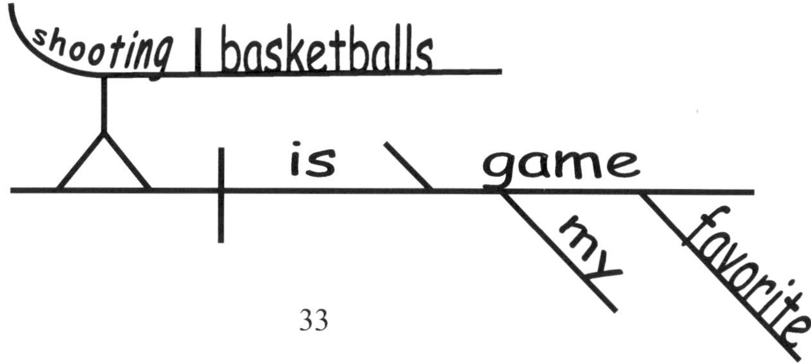

Taking walks is relaxing.

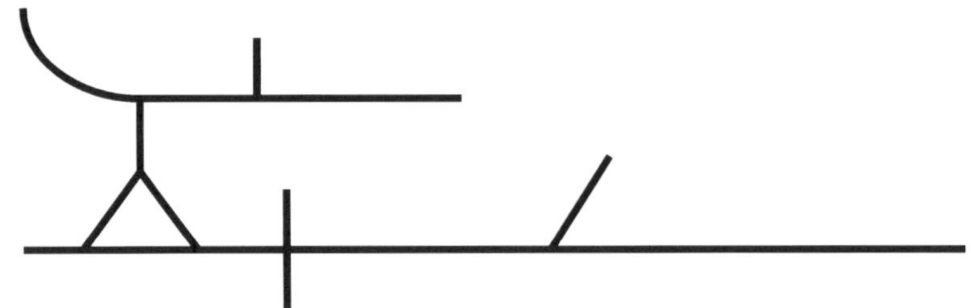

Decorating cakes takes patience.

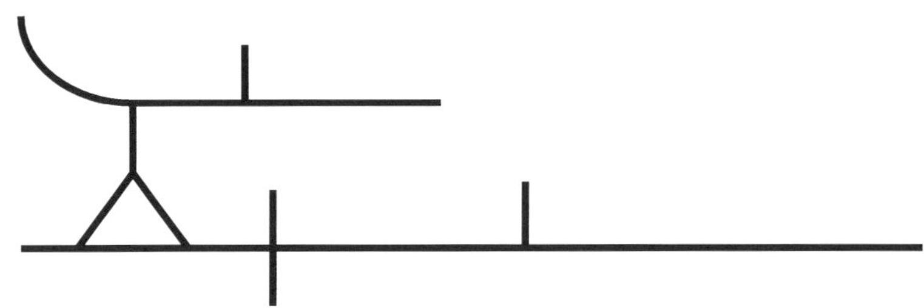

CLUE for gerunds
Verb acting as a noun

B

6. Relative Clause
As subject or direct object

RELATIVE PRONOUN

You learned about personal pronouns earlier in this module. There are other types of pronouns as well. A relative pronoun begins a relative clause. See the examples below.

CLUE

> Who
>
> Whoever   *Whomever*
>
> Whose
>
> Which
>
> Whichever
>
> That

Right now, we will focus only on relative clauses that act as the subject or the direct object.

Whoever runs fastest will win the race.

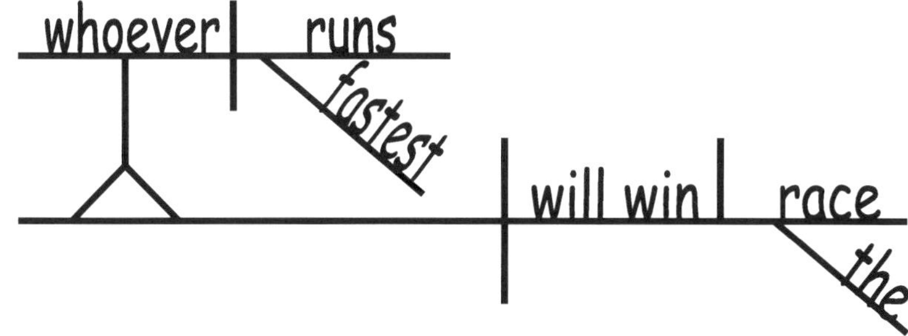

Whoever thinks kind thoughts is kind.

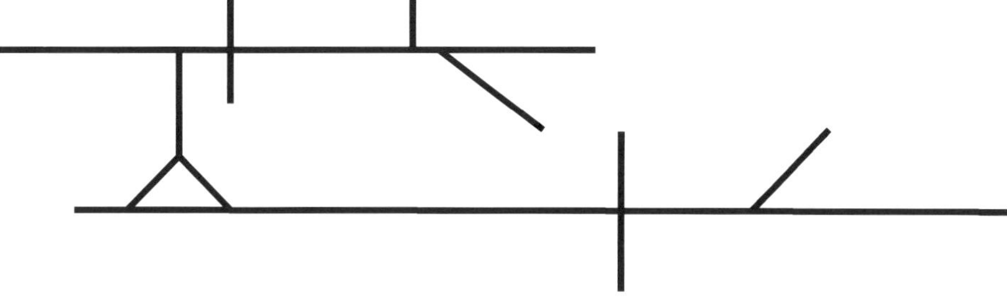

We will buy whichever is cheapest.

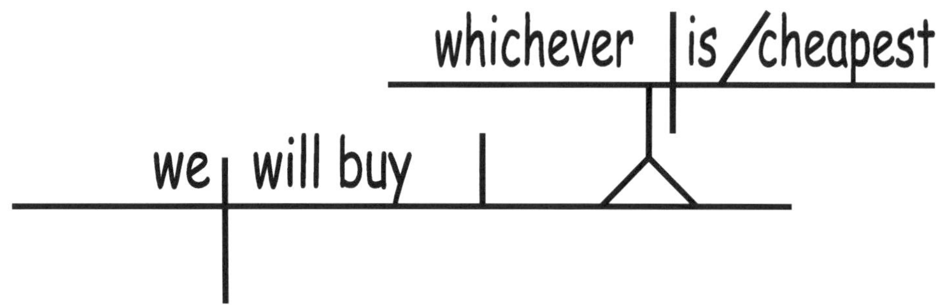

You should find who can come.

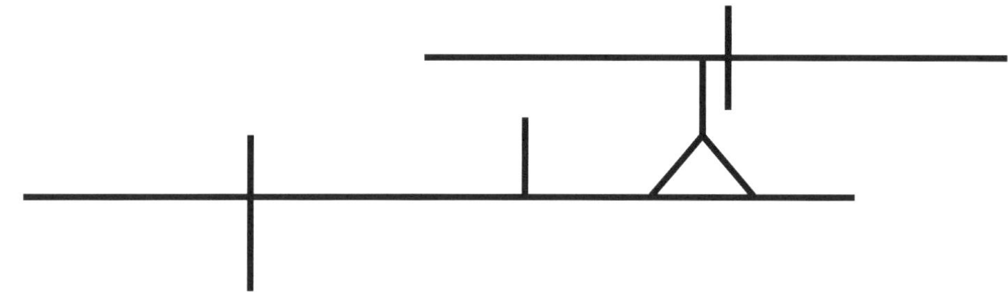

DIAGRAMMING
Although a relative clause is not a complete sentence, you should diagram it the same way a sentence is diagrammed. Look for the subject, verb, and any predicate parts.

Then, the relative clause will be put on the main frame with a stick figure as shown above.

ONE MORE THING – VERB PHRASES
The sentences above have a verb phrase, which is a group of words functioning as a verb. You will see in Module D why verb phrases are necessary in order to communicate more accurate and complex information. For now, recognize that phrases like "is looking," "has been sleeping," "might be running," or "should be cleaning," are all verb phrases that are diagrammed on the main line.

THE BIG BAD GRAMMAR SLAMMER

Module C   *Adjectives*

1. Simple Adjectives

An adjective modifies a noun.

It can fit in this space:

> The __________ puppy

It can describe, identify, or tell how many of a particular noun.

It can modify nouns that are the subject, the direct object, indirect object, predicate nominative or object of a preposition (which you will learn about soon.)

DIAGRAMMING

The adjectives are placed on a line under the main frame, below the noun they modify. They are diagrammed in the same way that articles (the, a, an) and possessive pronouns (my, your, our) are diagrammed.

The search party found the lost child.

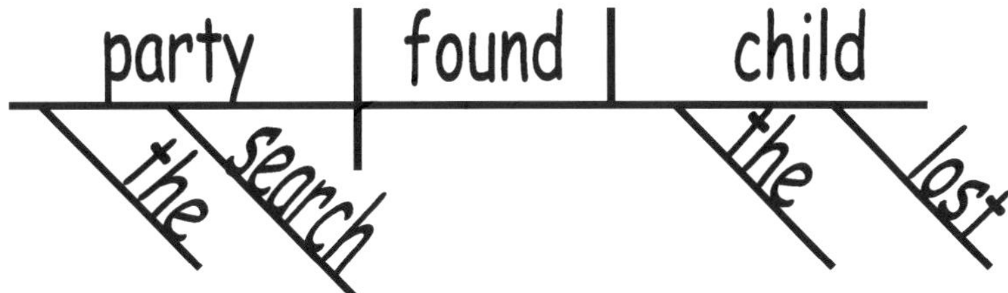

That pink gown is my favorite dress.

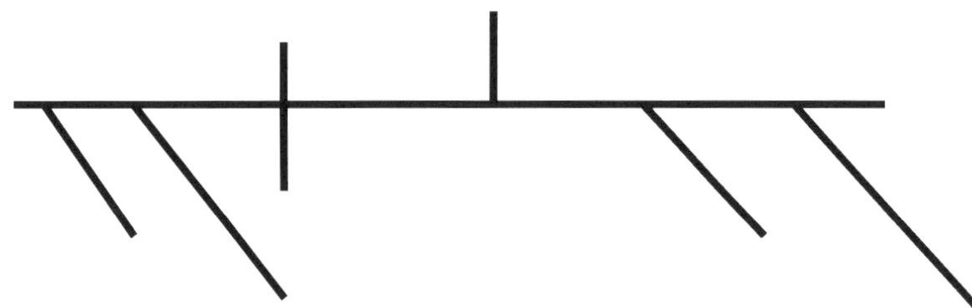

The little town gave their popular mayor a big surprise.

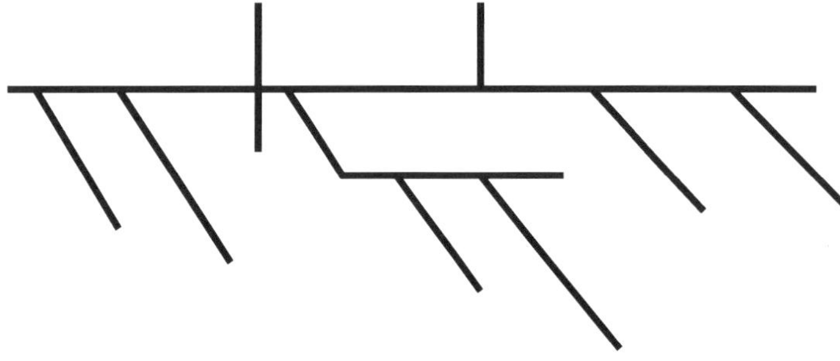

2. Prepositional Phrases
As Adjective Phrases

A phrase is a group of words that do not express a complete thought and do not have a subject and verb.

A prepositional phrase is a group of words that start with a preposition.

PREPOSITIONS				
About	Before	Down	Like	Through
Above	Behind	During	Near	To
Across	Below	Except	Of	Under
After	Beside	For	Off	Until
Among	Between	From	On	Up
At	By	In	Over	With
				Without

To remember the prepositions, you might find it helpful to divide prepositions into three types:

position in space	(in, under, near)
position in time	(after, before, during)
others	(to, by, of, with, from, except, like)

Use different colored pencils or highlighters to identify the three different types of prepositions above. This may make it easier to remember them.

ADJECTIVAL PREPOSITIONAL PHRASES
The preposition serves as an adjective (modifying a noun) if it modifies the noun. Consider the difference in these two sentences:
The dog in the car slept.
The dog slept in the car.

The prepositional phrase is the same in both sentences: in the car. In the first sentence the prepositional phrase acts as an adjective because it modifies the noun. It tells you which dog slept.

The prepositional phrase in the second sentence is not an adjective phrase, because it does not modify the noun.

OBJECT OF A PREPOSITION

The object of the preposition is a noun that follows the preposition to make a prepositional phrase. In the following phrases, the preposition is bolded and the object of the preposition is italicized.

> **under** the *bed*
> **by** the *car*
> **of** the *people*

QUICK CHECK

Just for fun, you might want to use the list of prepositions above, and verbally go through the list top to bottom and make up a prepositional phrase. See how fast you can go through the list.

DIAGRAMMING

Prepositions are diagrammed by a line going down from the main frame, under the word that is modified. The object of the preposition is written on an attached horizontal line.

The dog in the car slept.

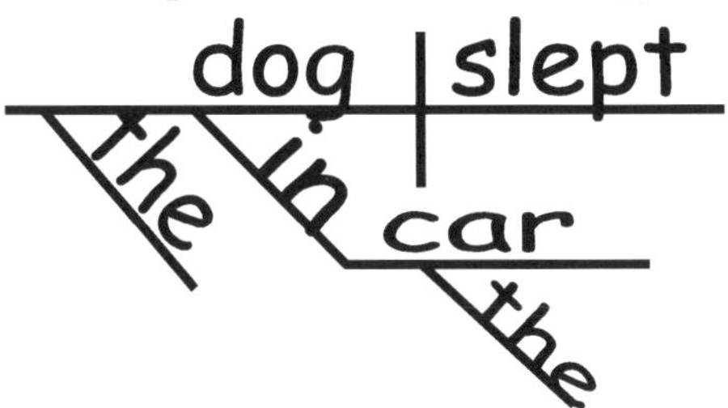

The frog in the creek was croaking.

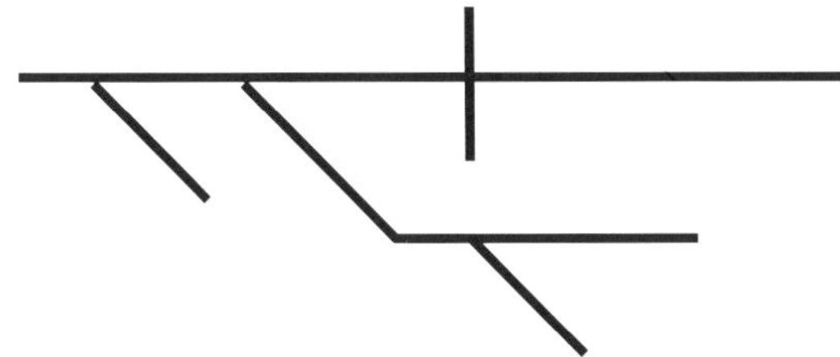

ADJECTIVES IN THE PREPOSITIONAL PHRASE
The object of the preposition may have an adjective, which will be diagrammed the same as a simple adjective.

The dog under the blue chair is sleeping.

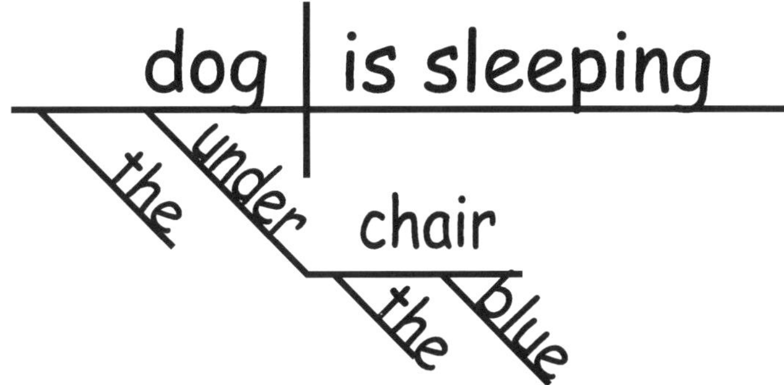

The yellow caterpillar climbed the wall behind the garden porch.

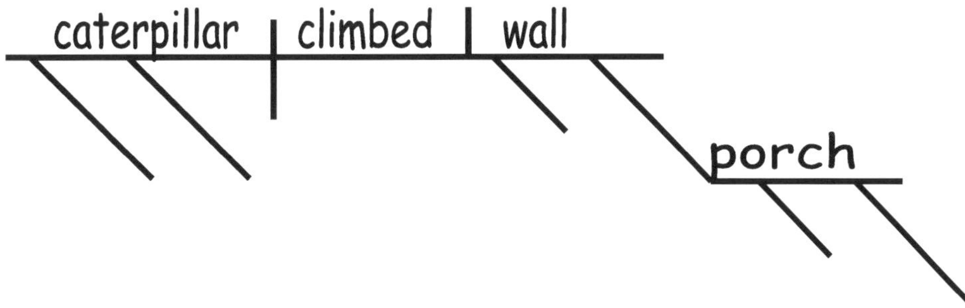

The stars in the night sky bring peace.

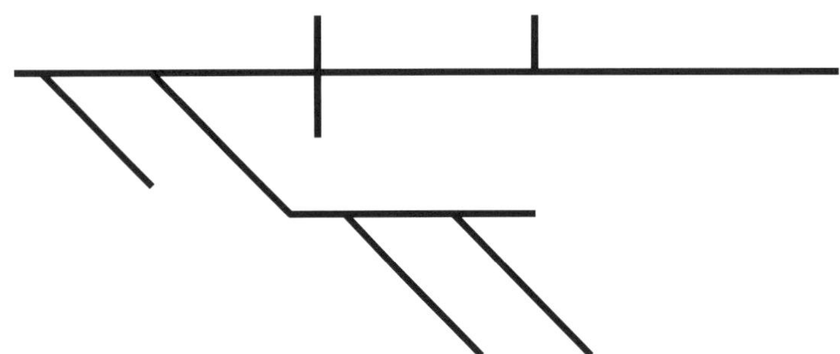

3. Compound Adjectives

If two adjectives both describe the same noun, they are compound adjectives.

The white, furry kitten meowed.

(White and furry both describe kitten.)

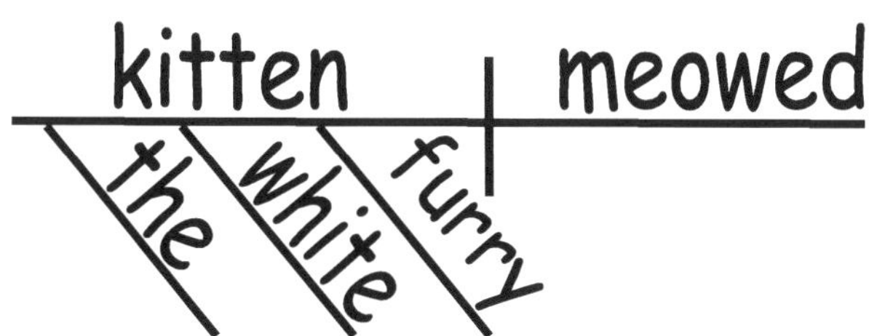

PUNCTUATION PEST

(Another pesky rule!)

You will need either a conjunction or a comma between the two compound adjectives.

The little, green bug flew.

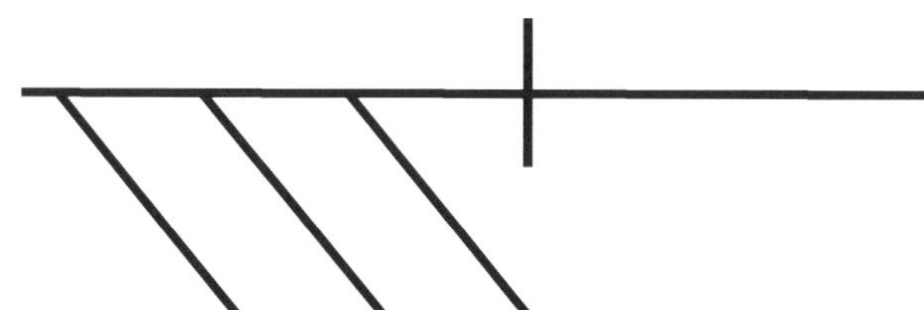

The smart and cunning fox stole the chicken.

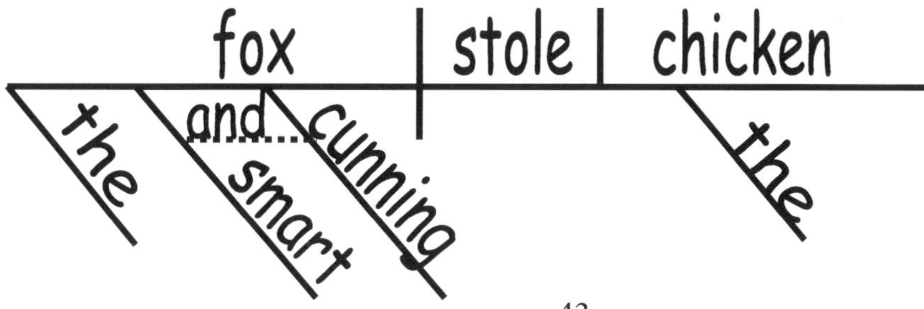

We like spicy and tangy foods.

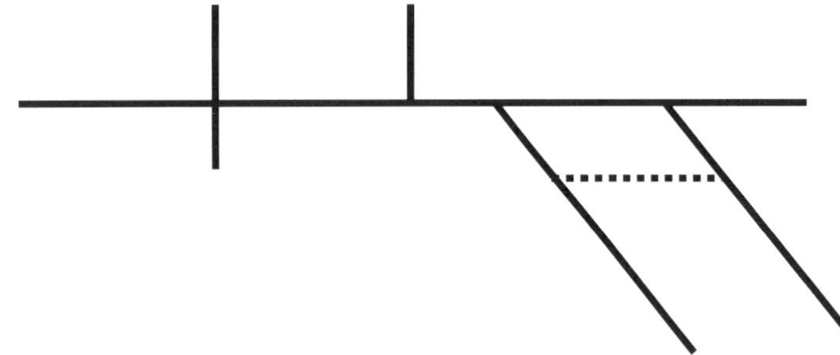

The river flowed through the quiet, charming village.

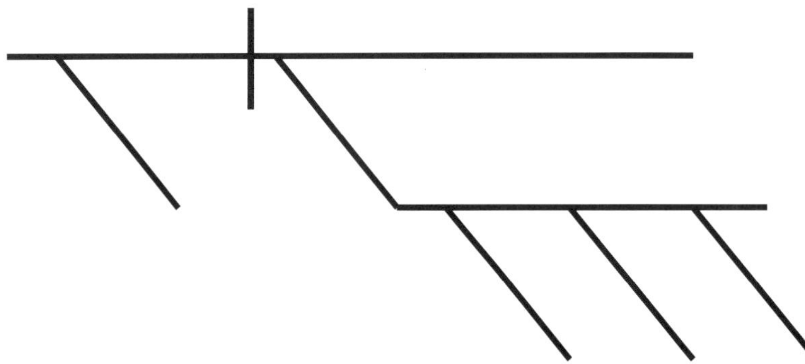

4. Participial Phrases as Adjectives

A participle is a verb form that is used as an adjective.

Baking cakes, my mother became tired.

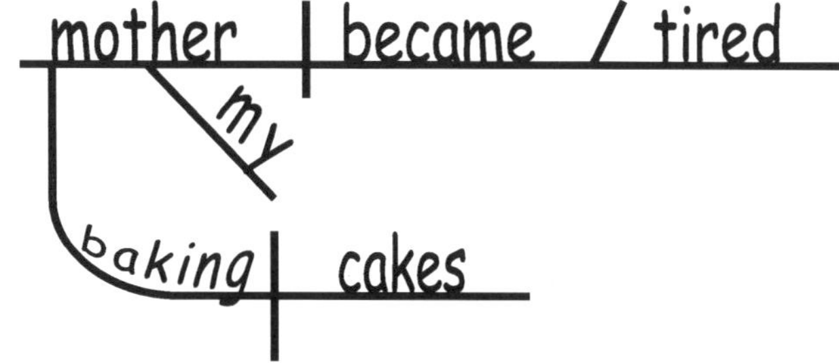

Sleeping in bed, the exhausted man was snoring.

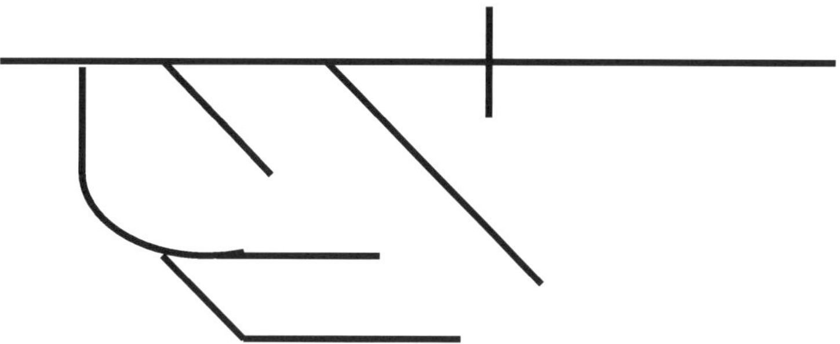

Finding the missing sheep, the shepherd rejoiced.

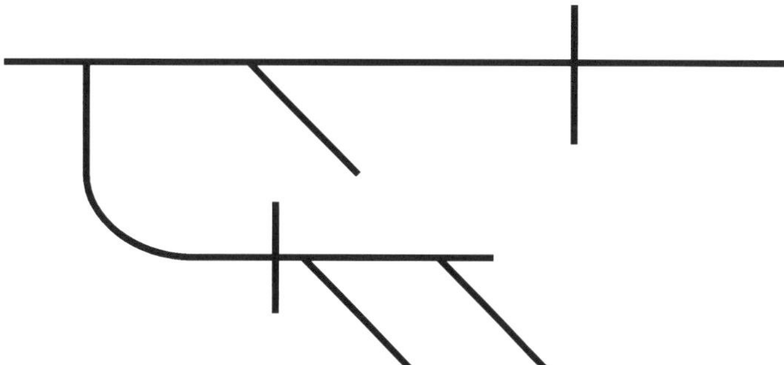

DIAGRAMMING PARTICIPIAL PHRASES

The participle is diagrammed with a curved line extended from the word it modifies. If there is an object of the participle, it will be placed on the other side of a vertical line. The diagramming for participial phrases is similar to the diagram for prepositional phrases, except a curved line is used.

5. Relative Clauses as Adjectives

A relative clause begins with a relative pronoun:
who, whom, which, whose, that

Comparison of clause and phrase:
Clause: Has a subject and verb
Phrase: Does not have subject and verb

CLAUSES	PHRASES
Relative That fell into the river Who found the house Which was broken	Prepositional Under the bed After the picnic For the children By the river Participial Thinking quickly Wandering slowly Aiming for the target

The child who was missing has been found.

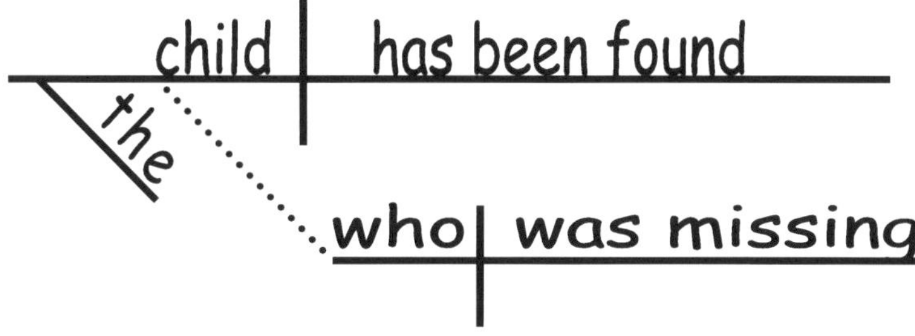

Diagramming
FIRST: identify the relative clause. In the example above,
the relative clause is "who was missing."

SECOND: determine the subject, verb and other word parts
of the relative clause. Diagram the relative clause.

THIRD: Identify and diagram the main skeleton of the
sentence:

FOURTH: Draw a line connecting the relative pronoun to
the word on the main frame that it modifies.

TRY THESE
I will share my recipe that won the contest.

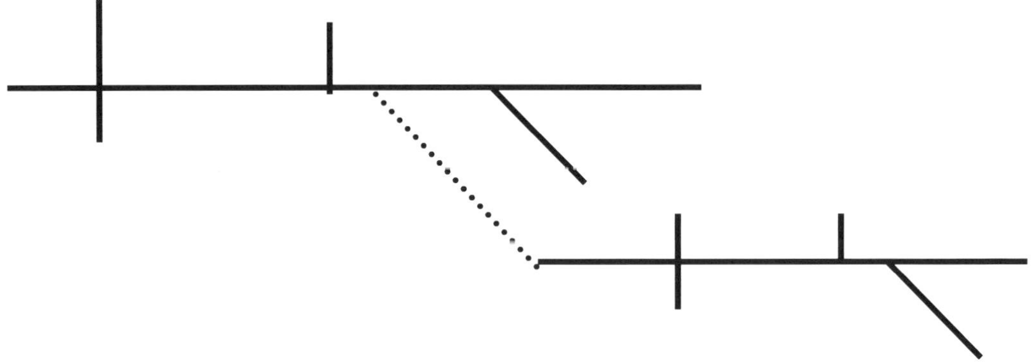

Teachers who motivate their students are successful.

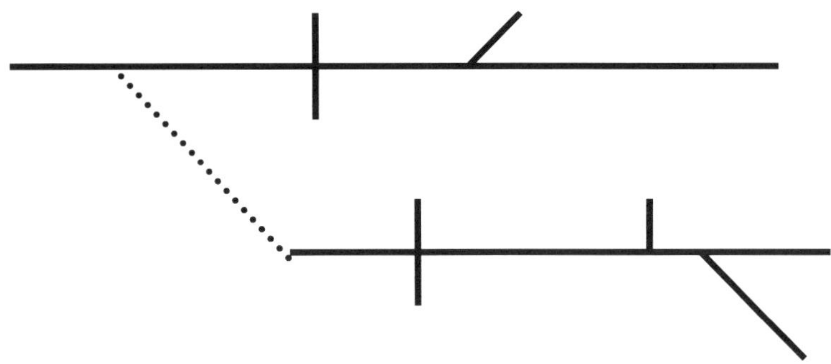

THE BIG BAD GRAMMAR SLAMMER
Module D   *Verb Tenses*

Do verb tenses make you tense?

Actually, you use different verb tenses throughout the day without being aware of it. It only seems complicated when you start giving names to the different tenses. But in reality, you are quite used to using future perfect tenses, even if you weren't aware of it.

BACK TO THE BASICS
Let's quickly mention the three most basic tenses: past, present, and future.

> **Past: I ran down the street.**
> **Present: I run down the street.**
> **Future: I will run down the street.**

I bet you can do this in your pajamas with one eye shut.

Now, it would be a bit easier to learn grammar if those were the only three tenses. However, you frequently communicate more sophisticated verbs than these three. So, the bad news is that you are about to embark on a short journey to unlock the mysteries of verb tenses. The good news is that they are based on the three simple tenses above (past, present, future.) If you have those three down, you are ready to begin.

1. Present Perfect Progressive

Compare these two sentences:

The bird chirps.
The bird has been chirping.

The second sentence is a Present Perfect Progressive Tense.

What does that mean?
PRESENT – It is in the present tense. The action is happening now.

PERFECT – The verb phrase uses "has" or "have" before the action verb. Please note that these words are also part of the verb and are on the main frame.

PROGRESSIVE – The action is continuing. One can tell by reading the sentence that the bird didn't just give one little chirp and then quiet down.

WHY?
While it may seem more complicated, it allows us to communicate more complex thoughts. For instance, try communicating this thought without the perfect and progressive tenses:

That noisy, little bird has been chirping (for the last three hours.)

Note: The parentheses indicate that you have not learned how to diagram this phrase yet. For those of you smart cookies that really want to know, it is an adverbial prepositional phrase and will be covered in Module E. Actually, it is a lot harder to say; and even harder to spell, than it is to do; so don't lose any sleep over it. I'm only including them here because it helps to understand why we have different verb tenses.

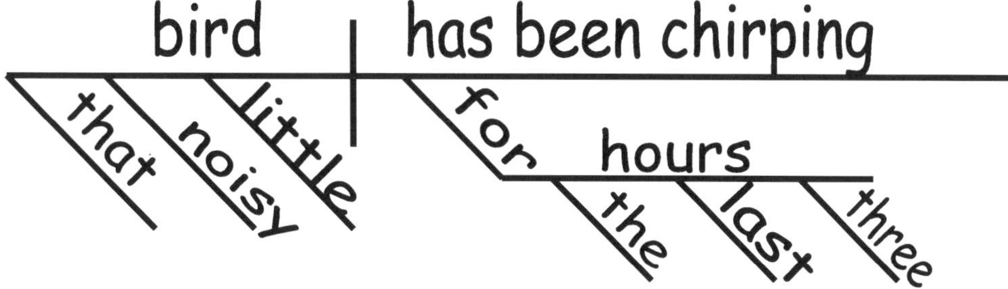

Here are a few others for you to study and diagram before embarking on writing a few Present Perfect Progressive sentences of your own.

The man has been mowing his lawn (since dawn.)

Our red car has been running (for five years.)

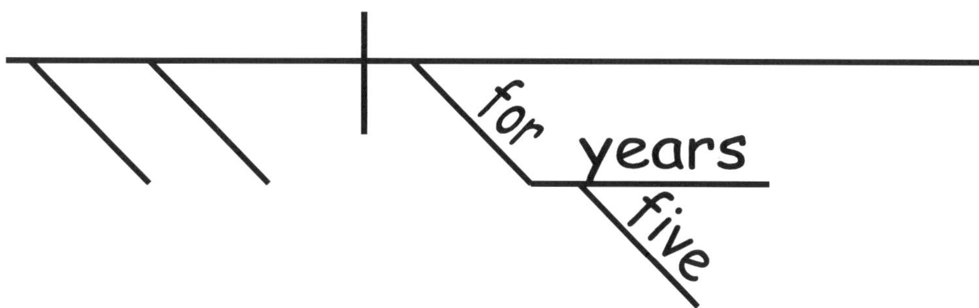

Do you notice how the action is on-going? It is taking place now (present), but it is not a single action that is once and done. (Instead it is progressive.)

2. Past Perfect – Simple Action

PAST tense is easy to recognize. It refers to action that took place in the past.

You are familiar with the PERFECT tense. It requires "has," "have," or "had" to complete the verb phrase.

SIMPLE ACTION can't be too complicated. It means an action that is done once, and then is finished.

So what could the little bird do with a Past, Perfect, Simple Action Verb?

The bird had chirped once (before he flew away.)

> Note: By the way, you will see some dependent clauses in parenthesis in the next few sentences. You haven't learned about them yet so you aren't expected to diagram them. However, these dependent clauses are helpful to show the value of the perfect tense.

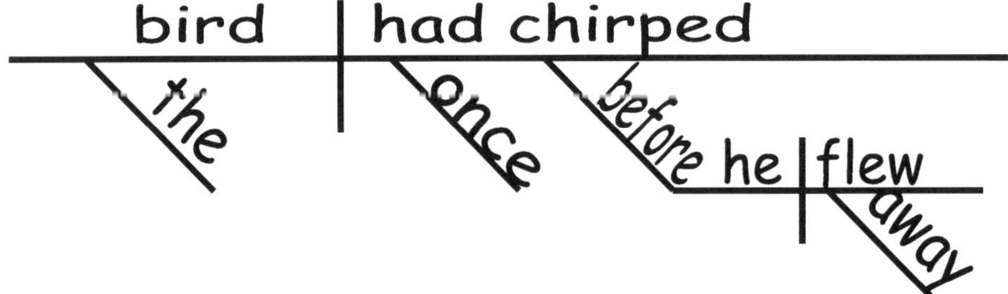

Here are a few others. Note they all have a simple action.

He had finished his lunch (before the bell rang.)

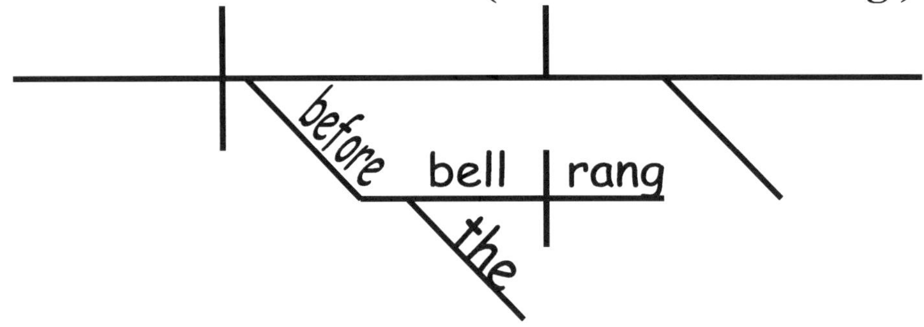

Mother had washed all my clothes (before I left.)

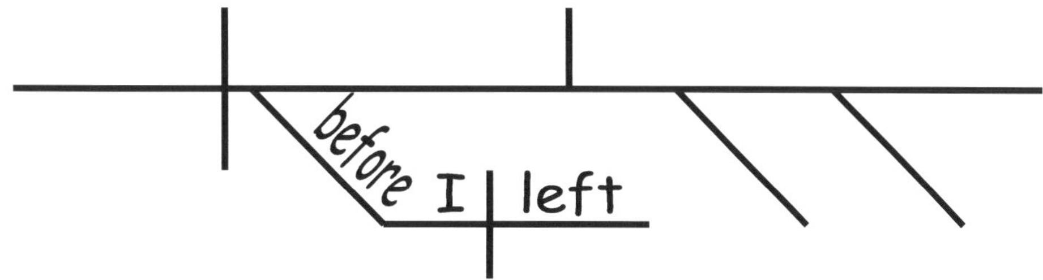

There is something you may have noticed. In many of these sentences, the past perfect verb tells an action that happened before another. That is the value of the perfect tenses. They can describe when one action happened compared to another.

3. Past Perfect Progressive

This really isn't so difficult once you get the hang of it. The Past Perfect Progressive is similar to the Past Perfect Simple Action except that the action is ongoing.

The bird had been chirping (for two hours before a cat climbed the tree.)

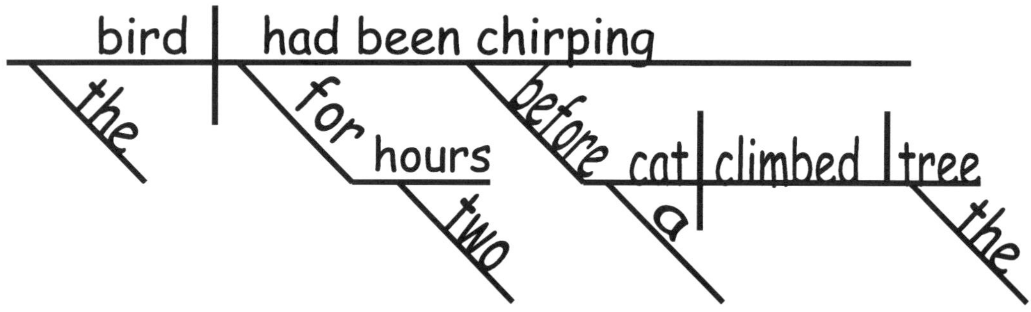

This tells you that the action is in the past, but it was an on-going action.   Of course, the action has since stopped, which is why it is past tense.

Let's try two more:
I had been searching my room (for an hour before I found my watch.)

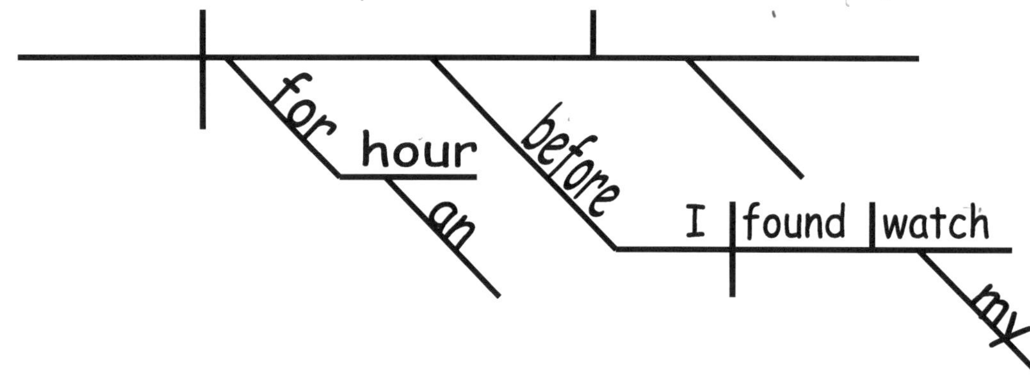

Greg had been hoping for a ride.

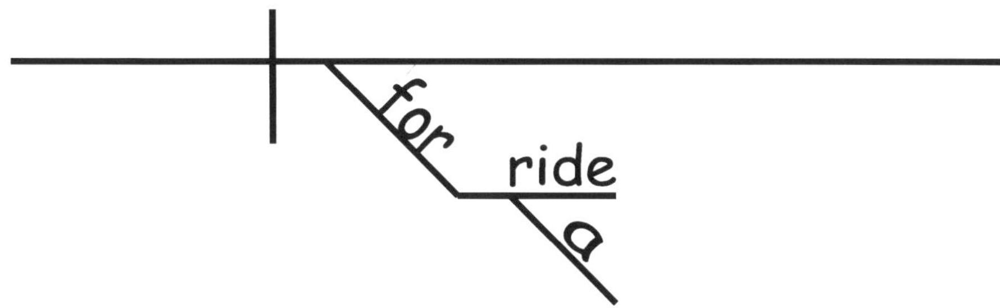

Hmm, in the last one you get the distinct idea that Greg is no longer hoping for a ride. It was a progressive, on-going action (hoping) that now has stopped (past.) So what do you think, did someone give the poor guy a ride?

4. Future Perfect Simple Action

My guess is that by this time you could probably write a sentence with a Future Perfect Simple Action without anyone having to explain it to you.

So let me ask you: How are these two different?
    Future Perfect Simple Action Tense
    Past Perfect Simple Action Tense

We will have eaten breakfast (before we ride to the post office.)

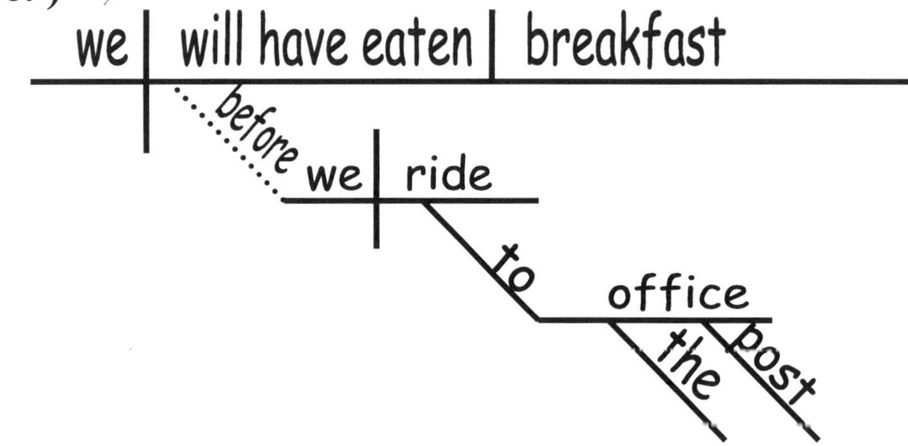

What is the value of this? Notice that the "will have + verb" communicates clearly several points:

- ➢ Both actions of eating breakfast and riding to the post office will take place in the future.
- ➢ The action of eating breakfast will have taken place, and be completed, prior to the next action of riding to the post office.

The city council will have voted (on the ordinance before the mayor speaks.)

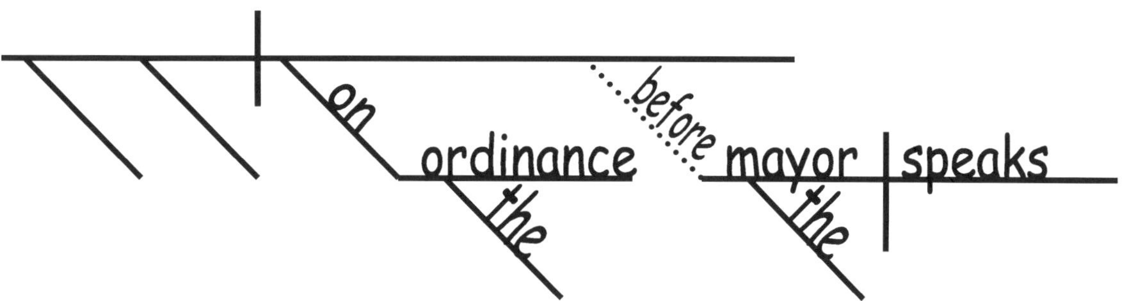

John will have wrapped the Christmas presents (before the tree is decorated.)

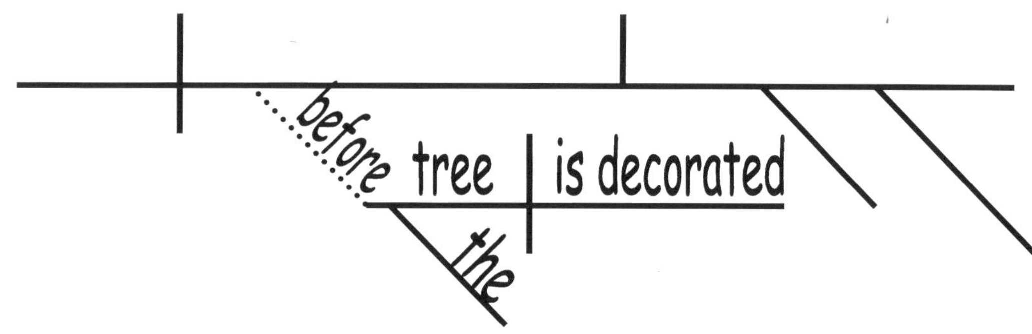

5. Future Perfect Progressive Action

This is similar to the last tense except – you guessed it – the action is ongoing.

By the end of August, we will have been traveling for three weeks. (This was said in June.)

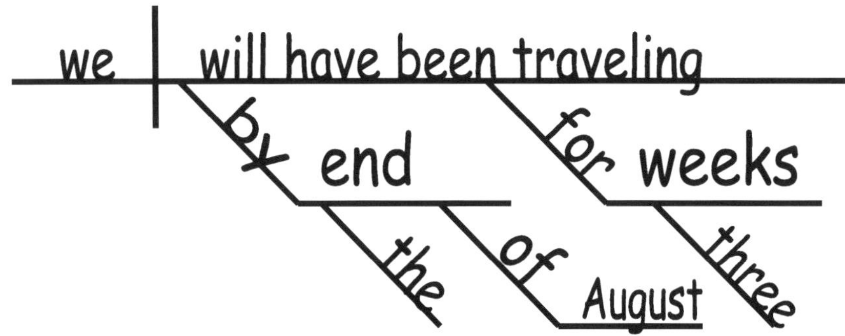

Here's another one:

The brownies will have been cooking (for twenty minutes before you take them out.)
This was said before they were even mixed

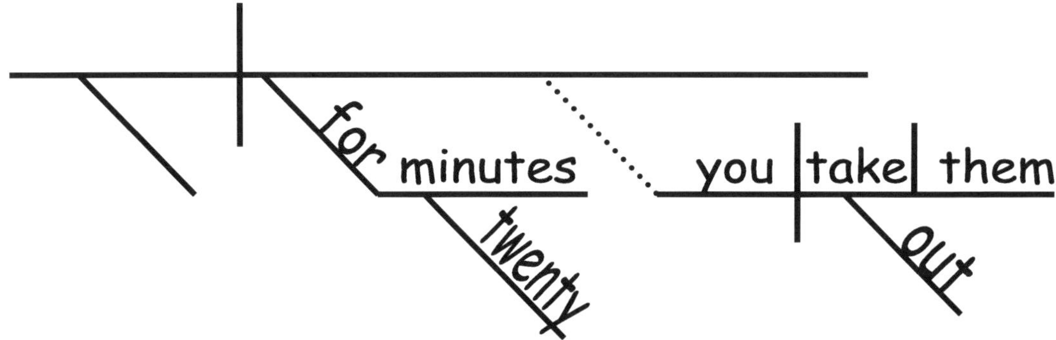

And what about our pesky little bird?

(By winter time,) that irritating bird will have been chirping (outside my window for eight months.)

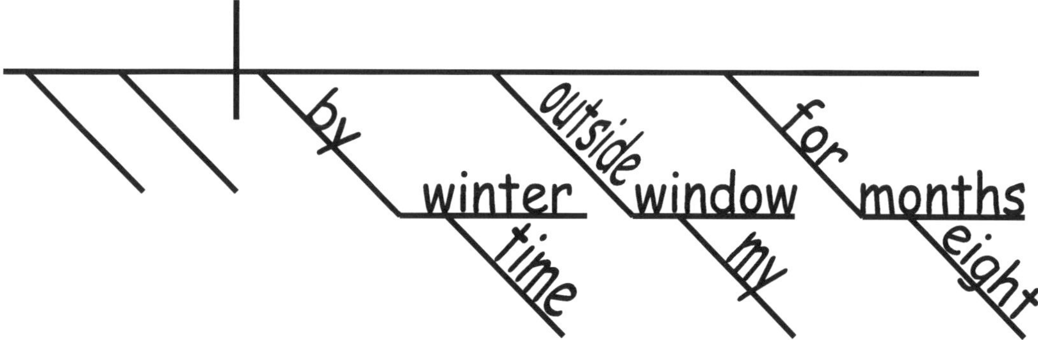

(Actually, I like to hear birds singing, so it wouldn't bother me at all.)

THE BIG BAD GRAMMAR SLAMMER

Module E   *Adverbs*

Introduction to Adverbs

An adverb modifies a verb, an adjective, or another adverb.

Say that again?

An adverb modifies:

> 1. a verb
> 2. an adjective
> 3. another adverb

If that seems confusing, just remember that adverbs can modify three different parts of speech, and you will know them by the time this module is complete.

Meanwhile, you should know this:

An adverb answers thcsc qucstions:

> ### *When?*
> ### *Where?*
> ### *How?*
> ### *How much?*

Go ahead; recite those four questions until you can chant them in your sleep.

Here's your clue:

> W?W?H?HM?

That clue stands for when, where, how, how much?

1. Simple Adverbs

A simple adverb modifies an action verb. You will see in Clue Card E that only an action verb can be modified by an adverb. Adverbs do not modify linking verbs.

The child cried yesterday.

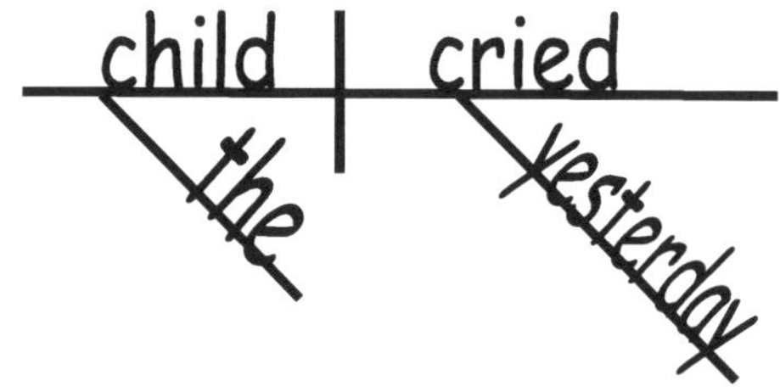

When did the child cry? Yesterday
Yesterday is an adverb that modifies the verb cried.

The child cried in the store.

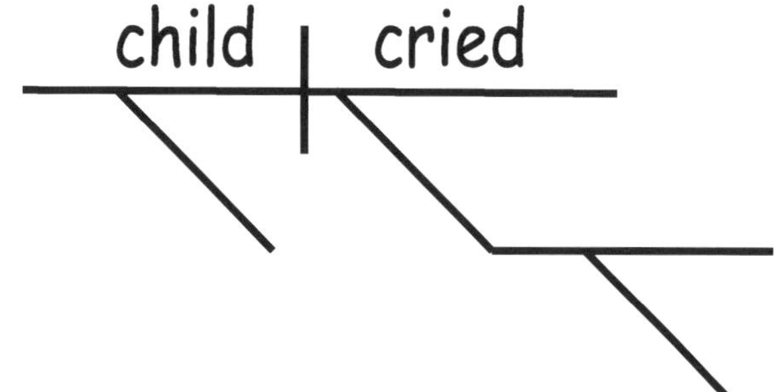

Where did the child cry? In the store

The child cried loudly.

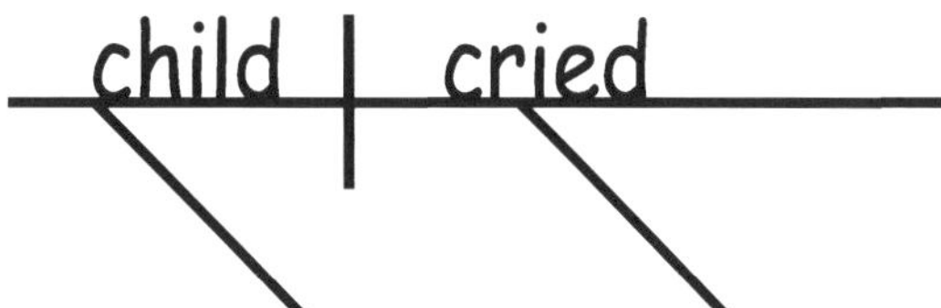

How did the child cry? Loudly

The child cried frequently.

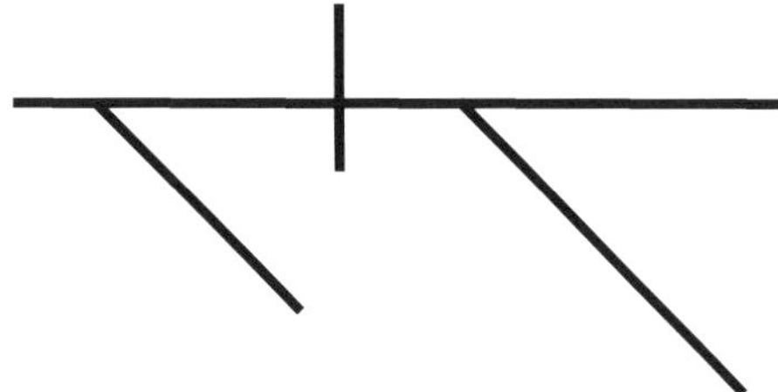

How much did the child cry? Frequently

DIAGRAMMING

The adverb hangs from the verb it modifies with a slanted line down.

He ate the sandwich hungrily.

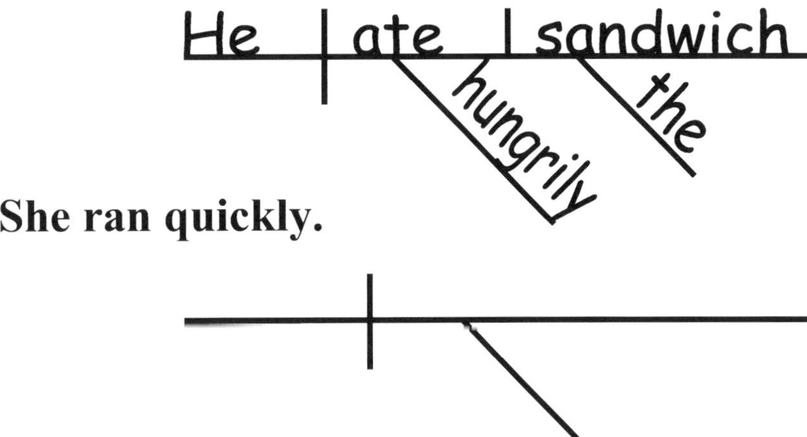

She ran quickly.

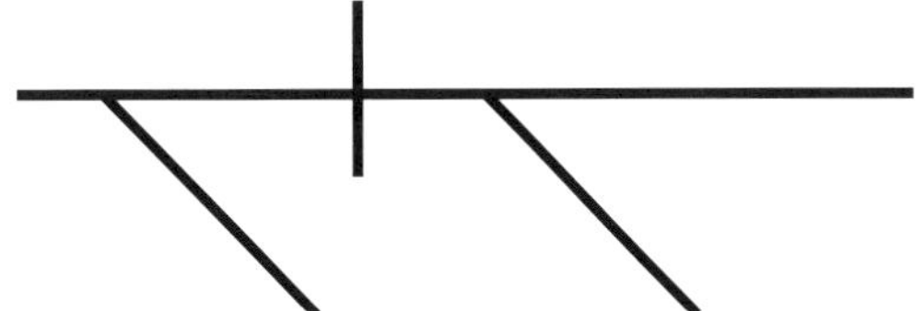

The dog bit hard.

2. Prepositional Phrases as Adverbs

You saw a few adverbial prepositional phrases in the last module. If a prepositional phrase modifies the verb, it is an adverbial prepositional phrase.

It will answer one of the four questions: W?W?H?HM?

What question do these adverbial prepositional phrases answer?

The deer ran in the forest.

The skier fell down the slope.

Remember, prepositional phrases give the position in time or space.

The businessman ate steak in the restaurant.

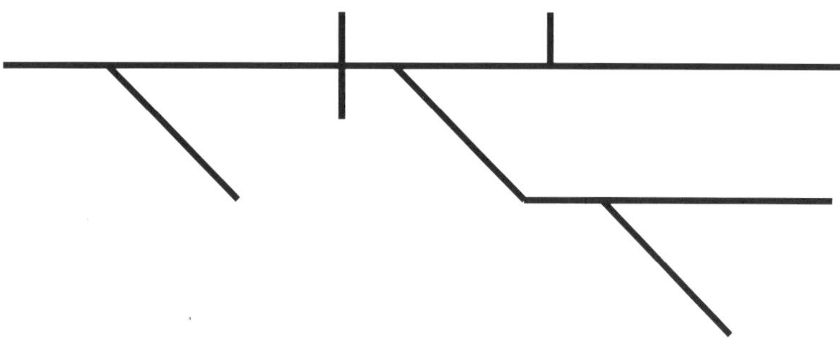

Notice the adverbial prepositional phrase does not always come right after the verb.

We will eat supper after the show.

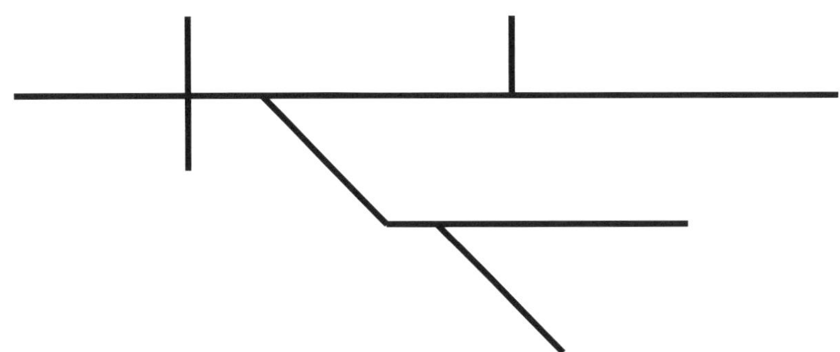

3. Adverbs modifying adverbs

An adverb can also modify another adverb. Read this sentence.

She sang very loudly.

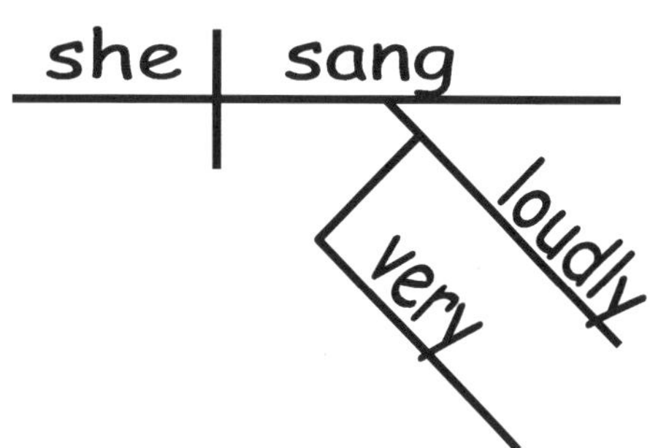

She sang *how*? Loudly is the adverb modifying sang.
How loudly did she sing? "Very" is the adverb modifying loudly.

DIAGRAMMING
To diagram an adverb modifying an adverb, draw a line off of the adverb and down parallel to it.

We ate really quickly.

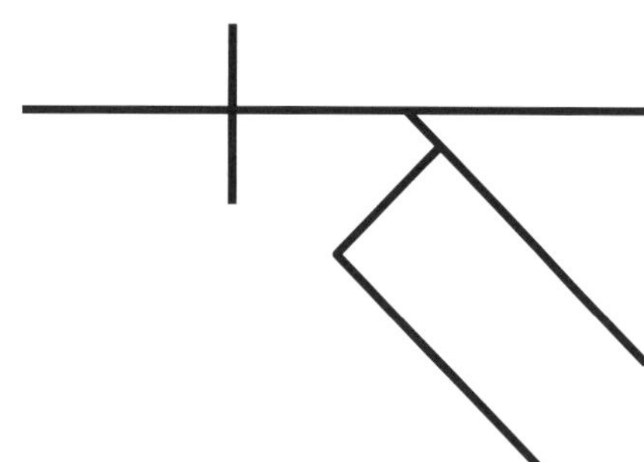

He studied quite seriously for his exams.

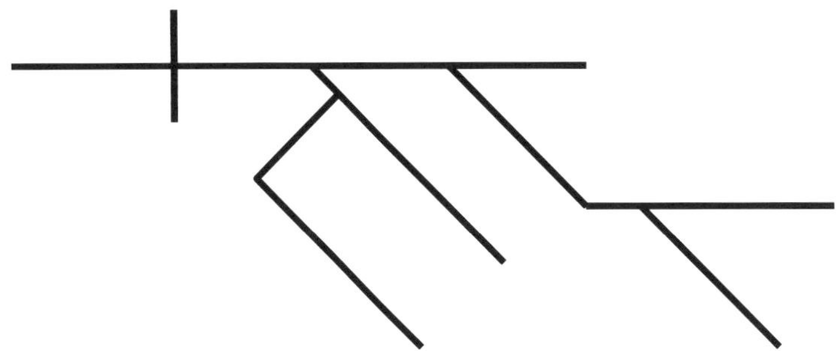

4. Adverbs modifying adjectives

An adverb can also modify an adjective.

The very wealthy man bought the bright green car.

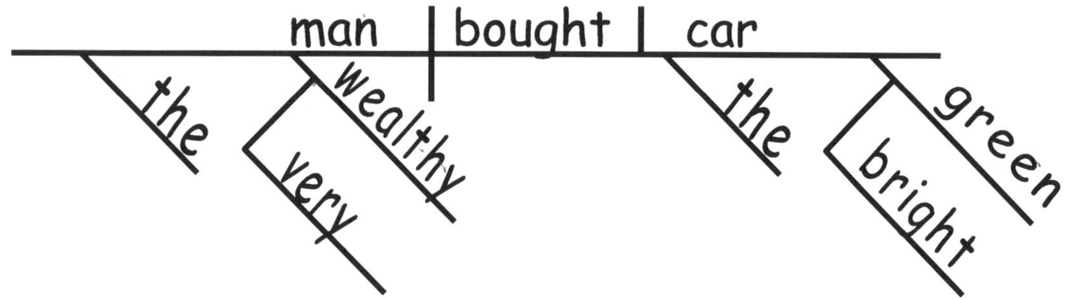

What does "very" modify? The adjective " wealthy."
Therefore "very" is an adverb.

What does bright modify? Since it modifies "green,"
which modifies "car," it is an adverb modifying an
adjective.

The extremely angry neighbor called the police.

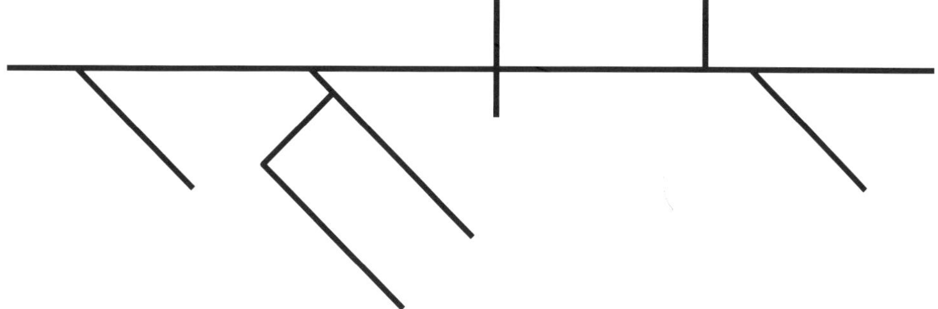

The police came quite quickly.

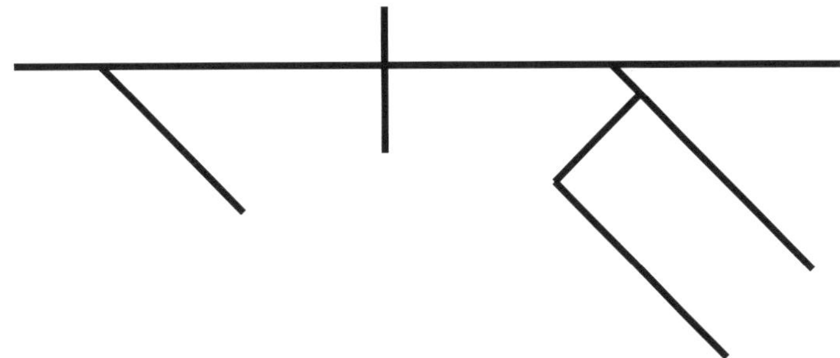

The neighborhood was perfectly peaceful.

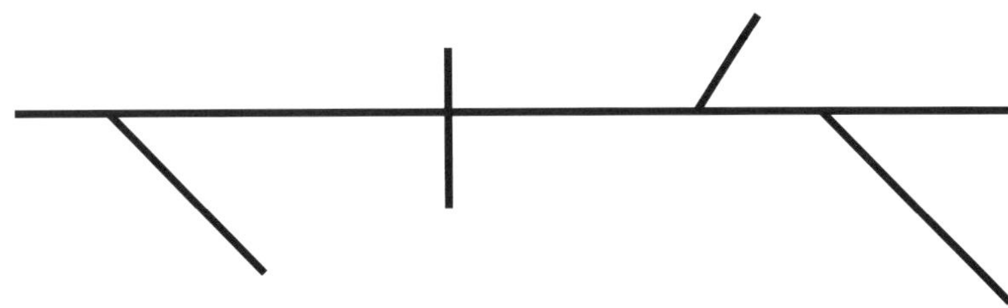

5. Complex Prepositional Phrases

If a prepositional phrase modifies a prepositional phrase, it functions as an adverb.

The car with the hole in the back drove away.

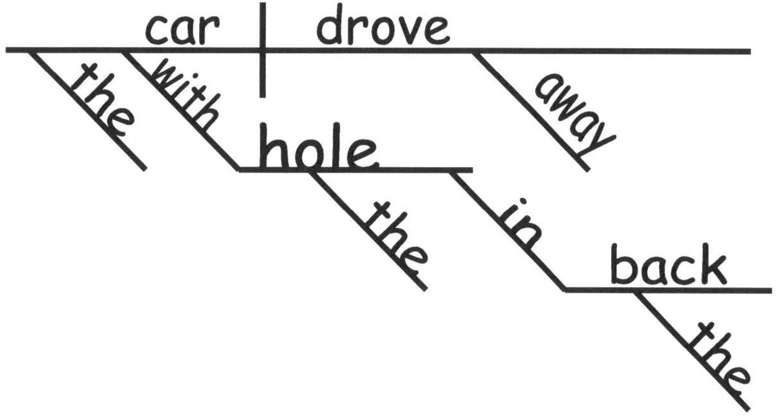

She found the ring with the diamond in the center.

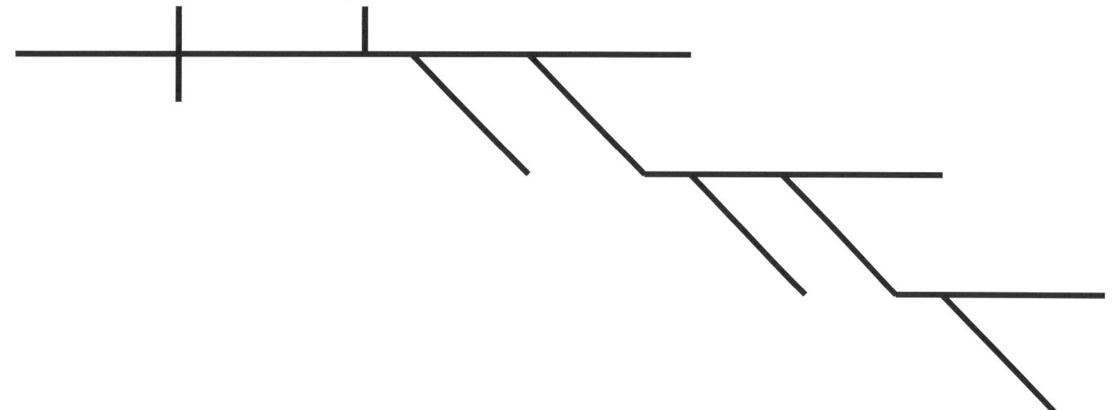

Actually, it is possible to get quite carried away with this. Just for fun, try the sentence on the back of this sheet☺

The branch on the tree in the back of the house by the corner of our road snapped off.

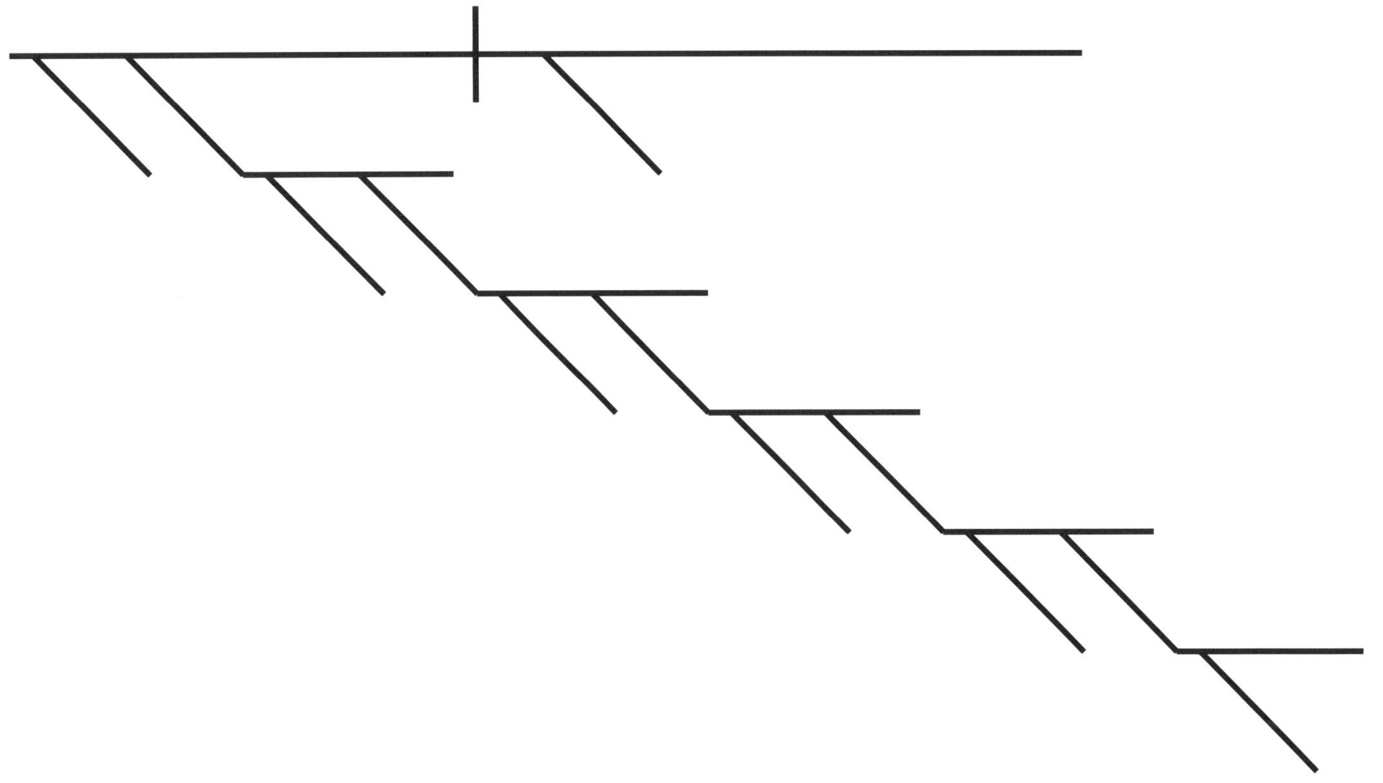

THE BIG BAD GRAMMAR SLAMMER
Module F   ***Miscellaneous Sentences***
1. Interjections

An interjection expresses surprise.

Wow! What was that?

DIAGRAMMING
The interjection is on a horizontal line in front of and separate from the main frame.

PUNCTUATION PEST 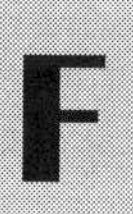

There will be an exclamation mark or a comma following the interjection. The exclamation mark is used in situations where extra emotion (surprise, anger, excitement, etc.) is expressed.

2. Direct Address

Direct address refers to the person's name that the sentence is addressed to.

Sheila, this is your coat on the floor.

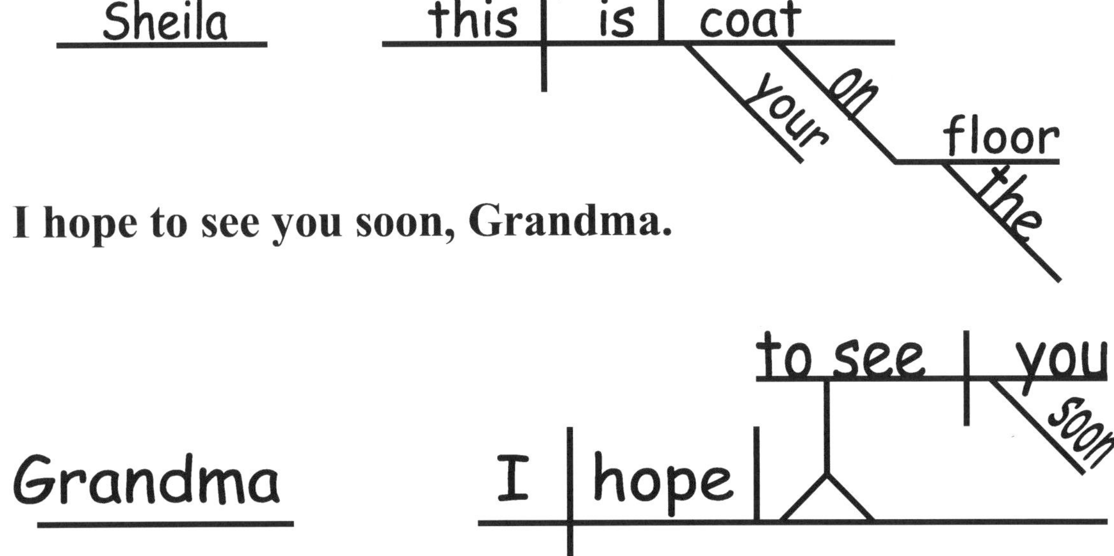

I hope to see you soon, Grandma.

DIAGRAMMING

The direct address is placed on a separate horizontal line in front of the main frame, similar to an interjection. Even if the direct address comes later in the sentence, the line will be put at the front.

Scouts, we will begin our journey now.
We will, Scouts, begin our journey now.
We will begin our journey now, Scouts.

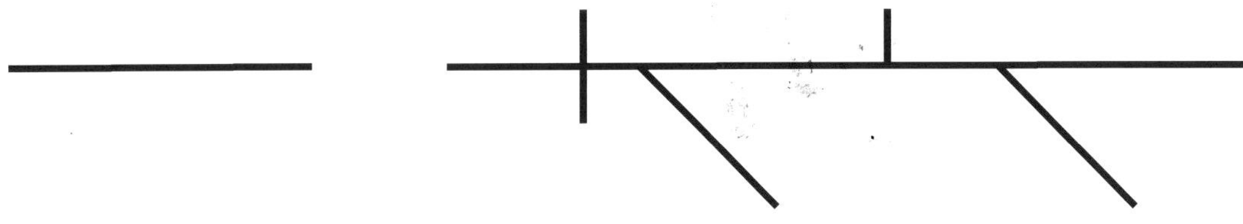

PUNCTUATION PEST

Always use a comma to separate the person's name from the rest of the sentence.

Double Whammy
Okay, Scouts, we will begin now.

Before we go on, it is time to mention imperative statements.
IMPERATIVE STATEMENTS

An imperative statement is a command. Imperative means "must", so it refers to something you must do. The subject of an imperative statement is understood to be "you." "You" refers to whoever the statement is addressed to.

For instance, with the sentence
Close your books.
The implied subject is "you" as in:
"You close your books."

DIAGRAMMING IMPLIED SUBJECTS IN IMPERATIVE STATEMENTS

The "you" is placed as the subject, but is in parenthesis showing it is understood. In some texts, an "x" may take the place of the word "you."

Triple Whammy
Okay, Class, close your books.

See, isn't this fun! Imagine that some people would rather spend time with their friends than do grammar!
(I dare you to diagram that!)

3. Direct Quote

A direct quote gives the exact words of the speaker as well as a tag telling who the speaker is.

All of the sentences below would be diagrammed like this:

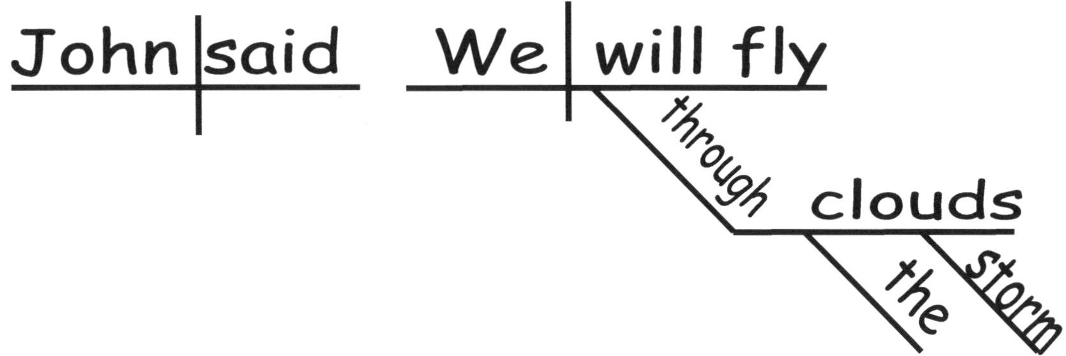

John said, "We will fly through the storm clouds."

"We will fly," said John, "through the storm clouds."

"We will fly through the storm clouds," said John.

 **PUNCTUATION PEST**

There is a comma separating the speaker tag from the quote, whether the tag is at the beginning, middle, or end of the sentence.

Capitalize the first word of sentences in a quote.

Do not use a capital in the middle of a sentence if the speaker tag comes in the middle.

Lori said, "We can have a picnic."

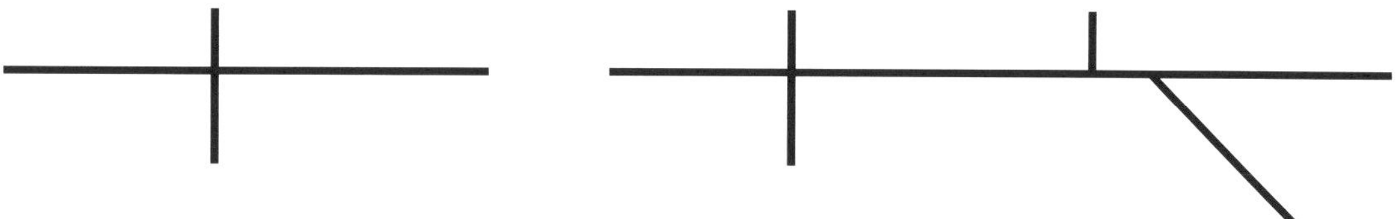

"We can grill steaks tonight," Dad said.

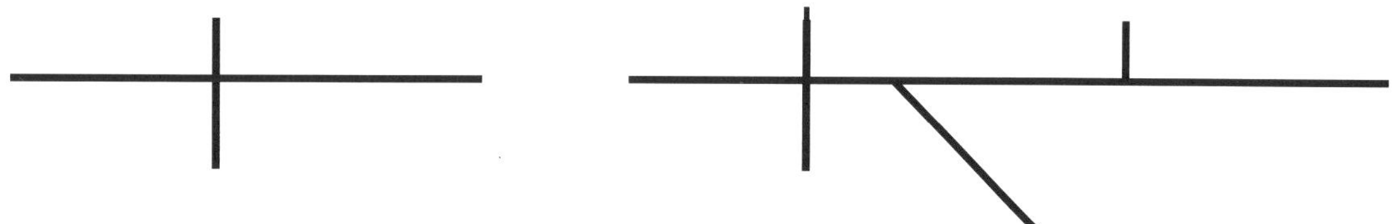

4. Interrogative sentence

An interrogative sentence is a question that splits the verb phrase.

Notice in the following sentences the verb phrase is underlined. It is split to change the sentence into a question.

I <u>am going</u> to the market.
<u>Am</u> I <u>going</u> to the market?

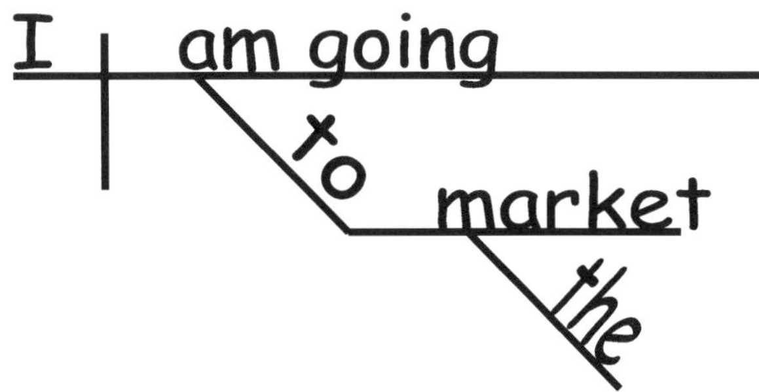

Someone <u>has been sitting</u> in my chair.
<u>Has</u> someone <u>been sitting</u> in my chair?

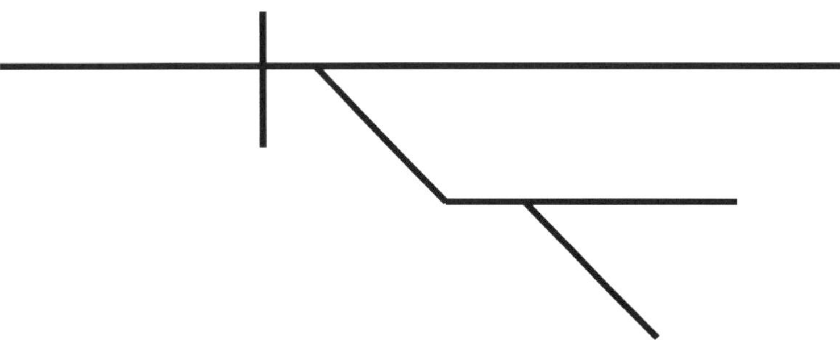

She <u>will be</u> my friend forever.
<u>Will</u> she <u>be</u> my friend forever?

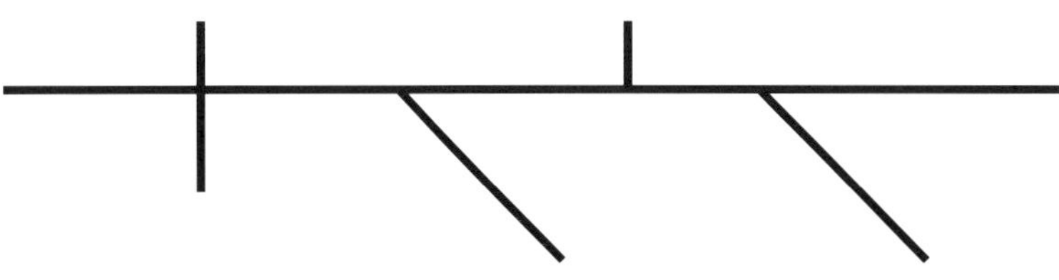

DIAGRAMMING

Diagram the interrogative sentence with the verb phrase intact. It will look the same as the declarative sentence the question was taken from.

Note:

Questions beginning with "who, what, when, why, how" do not follow the rule above. You do not need to know how to diagram these types of questions for this game.

5. Appositive

An appositive restates the noun to provide the reader with clarifying information.

Our first president, George Washington, has been called the father of our country.

Okay, we could diagram the main sentence simply enough:

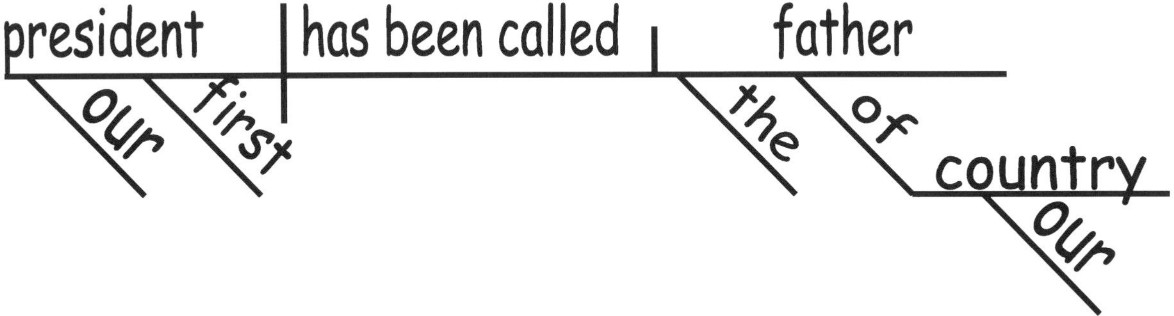

But what do we do with the name "George Washington?" Since the appositive restates the subject, it is put in parenthesis behind the subject on the main frame.

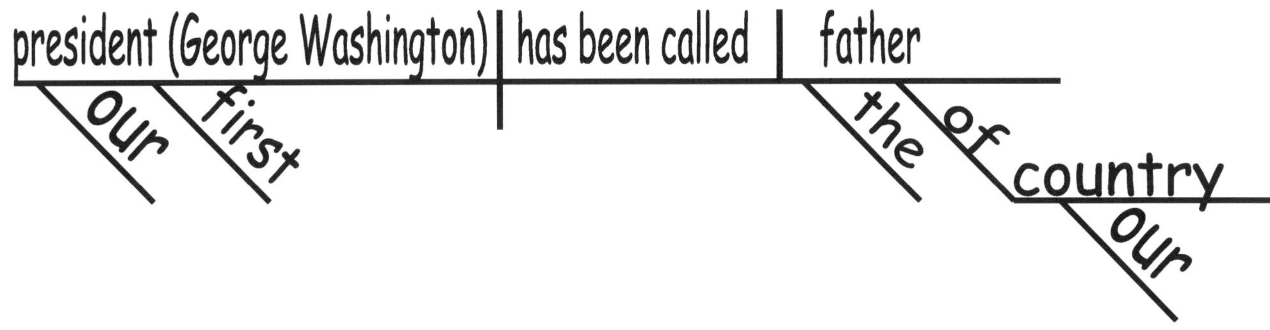

Of course, some people can get a little verbose as you can see in this appositive:

George Washington, the beloved first president of this noble land that is a beacon to all other nations of the earth, has been called the father of our country.

Relax, you don't have to diagram that sentence above. Instead, try diagramming this sentence with an appositive:

Mrs. Smith, my teacher, enjoys ancient history.

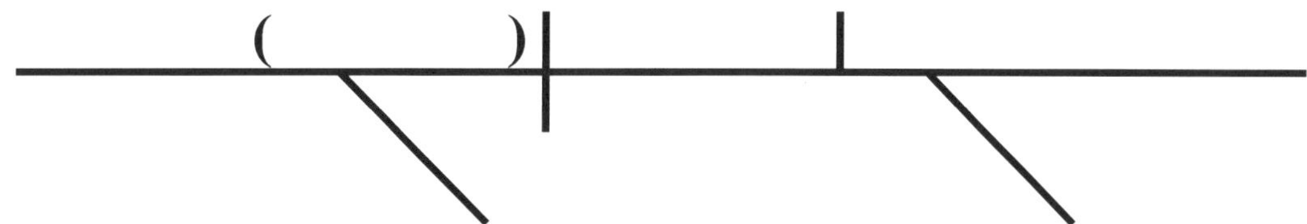

**Now, put on your grammar cap and get
ready for some real fun.**

THE BIG BAD GRAMMAR SLAMMER

Module G   ***Compound/Complex Sentences***

Introduction

I. COMPOUND SENTENCES

A compound sentence is a sentence that has two or more clauses, each of which could be a complete sentence grammatically.

Remember, you have seen compound subjects.

The boy and girl ran.

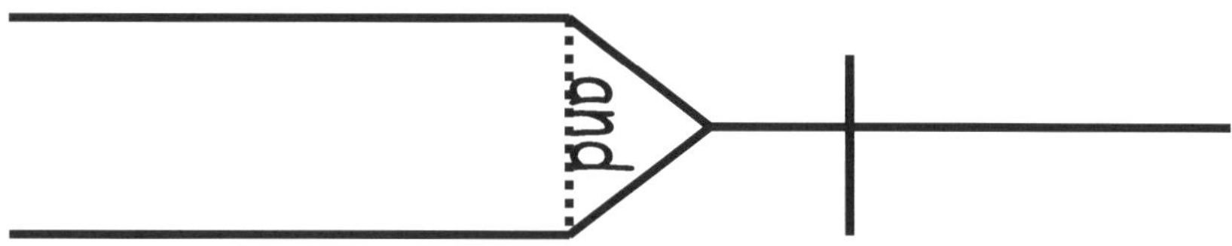

You have seen compound verbs:

The boy ran and jumped.

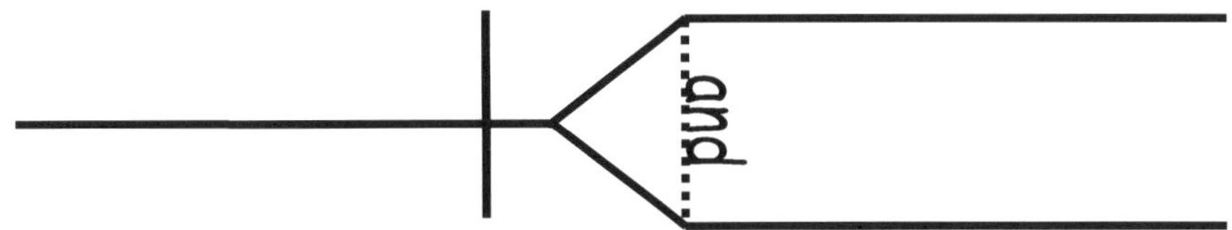

You can have compound direct objects:
The girl ate her cereal and toast.

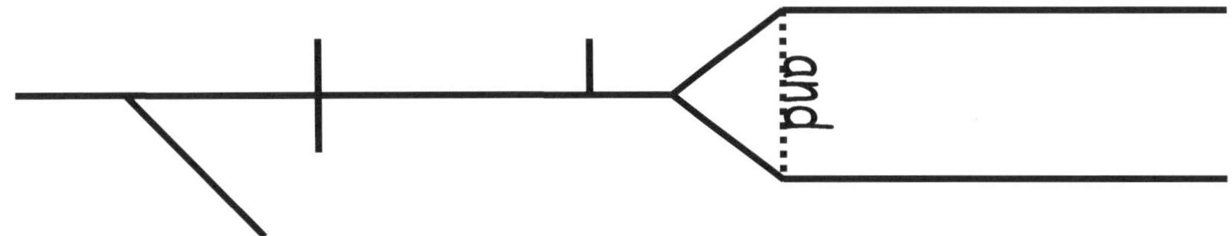

Well, why can't we have a compound sentence?
The girl ate her cereal, and the boy ate his toast.

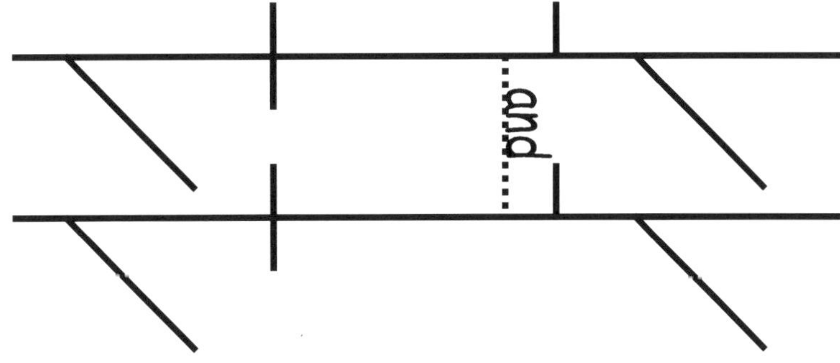

II. COMPLEX SENTENCES
A complex sentence has a clause that could not be a complete
sentence.

Because he was hungry, the boy ate his toast.
The second clause could be an independent sentence, but the first
clause could not. Viola! A complex sentence it is.

See that wasn't so hard was it? Complete this module with its five
rules for compound and complex sentences, and let
Mrs. Commafuss out of the Slammer.

Module G   *Compound/Complex Sentences*
1. Comma, Conjunction with a Compound Sentence
CS, and CS

Two clauses that could stand independently can be connected by a conjunction.

Common conjunctions:

      AND

        OR

          BUT

I am cold, but it is hot outside.

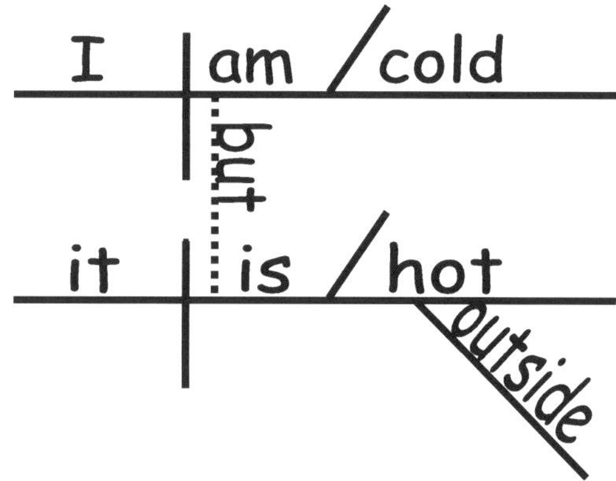

You can have peanut butter, or you can have grilled cheese.

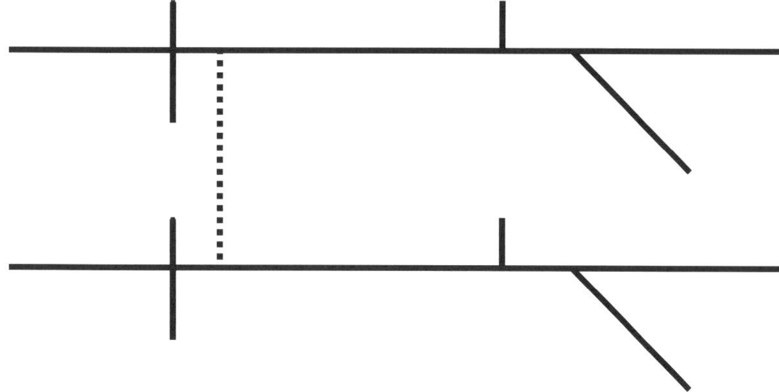

Steven is twelve, and his sister is fifteen.

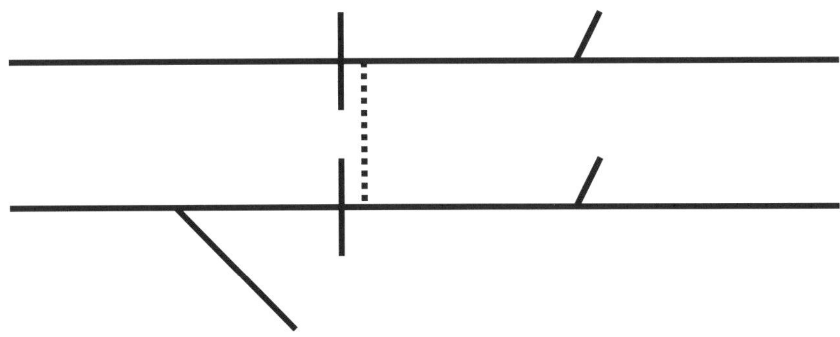

DIAGRAMMING

Connect the two verbs with a dotted line. Write the conjunction on the line.

PUNCTUATION PEST

Do you see why we call this rule Comma, Conjunction?
There is always a comma before the conjunction when two clauses that could be independent are joined to form a compound sentence.

CLUE

CS, and CS

The "CS" stands for "complete sentence." Now, I need to warn you that this is not strictly correct. You see, a true blue grammarian would call each of these an Independent Clause. Now, an Independent Clause is a group of words that COULD function as a complete sentence. Such grammarians, such as our dear Mrs. Commafuss, would insist that it is not a complete sentence, in that we have just put that group of words into a compound sentence. Therefore, the new compound sentence is the complete sentence, not the independent clause. However, you will learn that there are also dependent clauses (those are groups of words that CAN'T function as a complete sentence; they have to be dependent.) However, when you start talking about dependents and independents the two sometime get tangled up with each other, which may very well be one of the reasons some people have grammar nightmares and had Mrs. Commafuss thrown into the Grammar Slammer. So we think it's easier to call the things Complete Sentences (i.e. CS) if it could be a complete sentence. It makes it a bit easier to understand, and one less thing to learn. We do offer our apologies to all you certified, card-carrying grammarians out there who are offended by this, and hope you don't end up in the Slammer with Mrs. Commafuss.

(Hey, did you notice how I used a comma-conjunction with that last sentence?)

2. Compound sentence with a semi-colon
CS; CS

Two complete sentences can be combined with a semi-colon to form a compound sentence.

You just learned to combine two clauses that could be complete sentences with a comma and conjunction to form a compound sentence. Well, you could also combine those two sentences without the conjunction. In that case, you would use a semi-colon between the two clauses.

One year olds are babies; two year olds are toddlers.

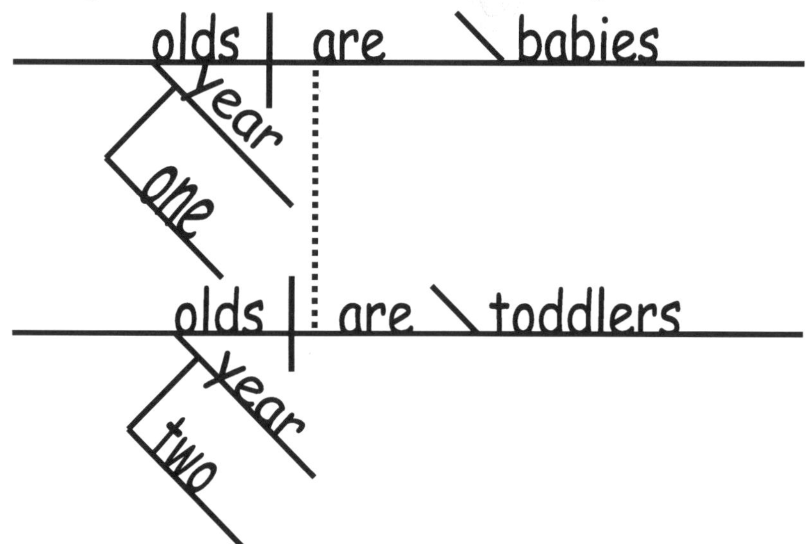

It is raining; you need an umbrella.

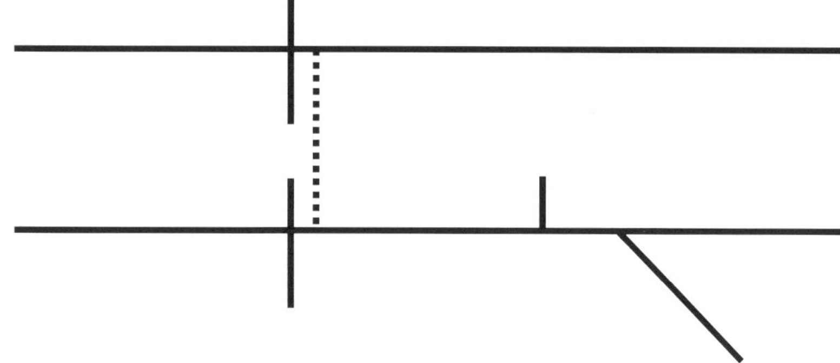

I want chocolate; I dislike vanilla.

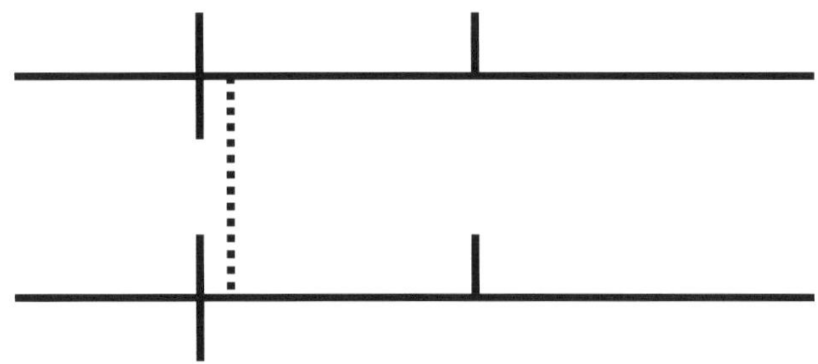

If the two sentences express a single thought, they can be combined into a single compound sentence. In the three similar sentences below, notice how the punctuation affects the sentences.

Steven is twelve. His sister is fifteen.
Steven is twelve, and his sister is fifteen.
Steven is twelve; his sister is fifteen.

The more closely you want to connect the two ideas, the closer they can be combined in a compound sentence.

DIAGRAMMING
These are diagrammed just like the compound sentences with a comma-conjunction. This time, however, we can't add the conjunction; it isn't there.

(Psst, I'm <u>sure</u> you caught the fact that the last sentence is a compound sentence with a semi-colon. Right?)

3. Complex sentences with a comma
sc DC, CS

It's really not that hard, but we'll take this concept a bit slowly.

FRAGMENTS or COMPLETE SENTENCES

I assume that somewhere in your past studies, you may have been like the majority of students who had to decide whether a group of words is a complete sentence or a fragment. Do you remember writing "F" for fragment or "S" for sentence in front of a list of clauses like this:

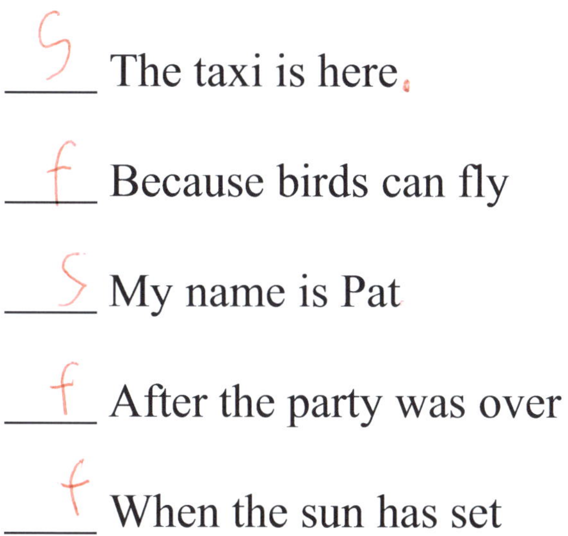

_____ The taxi is here.

_____ Because birds can fly

_____ My name is Pat

_____ After the party was over

_____ When the sun has set

Now, I'm going to make the assumption that you can readily tell the complete sentences in those examples above. Otherwise, the material to follow is going to be a bit over your head.

DEPENDENT CLAUSE (DC)

Those fragments listed above are actually dependent clauses. A dependent clause is a group of words that cannot function as a complete sentence. But there is one other thing that makes the dependent clause a dependent clause; it has a subject and verb. Notice all the examples above that are not complete sentences still have subjects and verbs.

SUBORDINATE CONJUNCTIONS (sc)

There is something else I want to point out about the examples above that are not complete sentences. If you took the first word away, the words would then make a complete sentence. There is a special group of words called **subordinate conjunctions** that turn complete sentences into dependent clauses. Here is a list of those tricky little words:

After	In order to	Until
Although	Since	When
As	So	Whenever
As soon as	Then	Where
Because	That	Whenever
Before	Though	Whether
If	Unless	While

Try it yourself. Take any complete sentence, slap one of these subordinate conjunctions in front of it, and – viola – you have a dependent clause. Pretty tricky, huh?

You may have figured out that the Dependent Clause is called so because it is unable to stand on its own, so it is depending on the Complete Sentence (CS) to make our sentence grammatically correct.   If so, congratulate yourself on your astuteness. Otherwise, read that sentence again.

So, let's give it a try here.
Whenever I finish dinner, I brush my teeth.

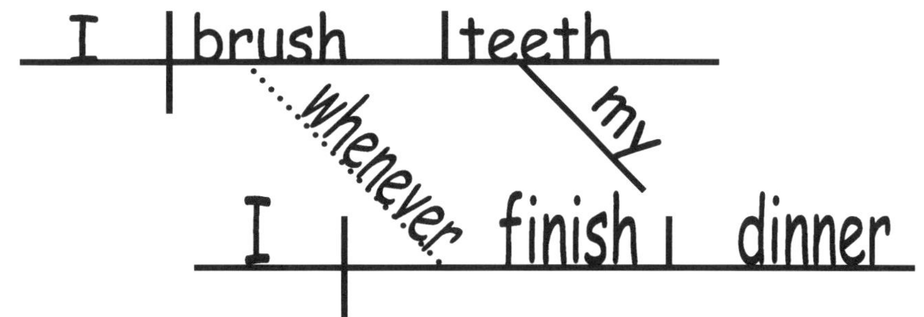

Because he had a cold, Roger stayed at home.

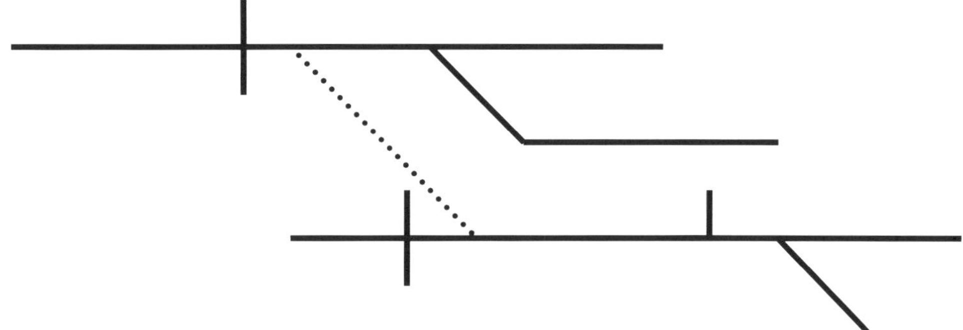

If you are a teenager, you cannot order from the children's menu.

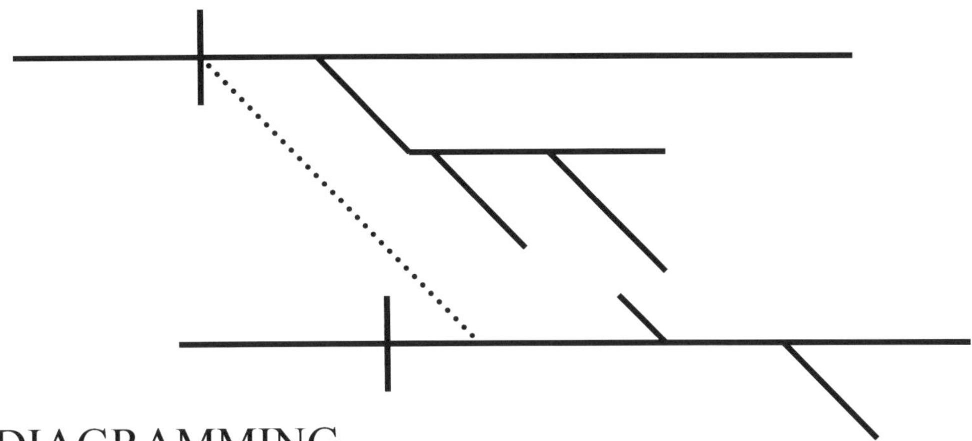

DIAGRAMMING

As you can see from the above examples, both clauses are diagrammed as complete sentences. The dependent clause is below and indented in from the complete sentence. A dotted line connects the two verbs, and the subordinating conjunction is written on the line.

PUNCTUATION PEST

If the subordinating clause comes before the complete sentence, a comma separates them. (I'm sure you noticed I used that rule in punctuating that sentence. You see, this stuff really does work!)

4. Complex sentences without a comma
CS sc DC

I sure hope you understood all that stuff about dependent clauses and subordinating conjunctions and complete sentences. If you did, you got past all the hard parts and its downhill from here.

On the other hand, if you didn't you may need to review the last two rules again, or this one is going to put both of us in the Slammer with Mrs. Commafuss.

In a nutshell, the two clauses that make up a complex sentence can be put in either order; the dependent clause can come first or the complete sentence can come first. The only difference is whether or not you need a comma.

For instance, compare these sentences with the sentences in Rule 3 of this module:

I brush my teeth whenever I finish dinner.

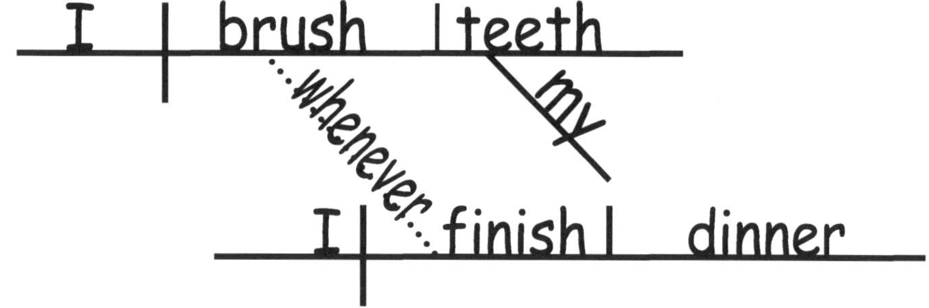

Roger stayed at home because he had a cold.

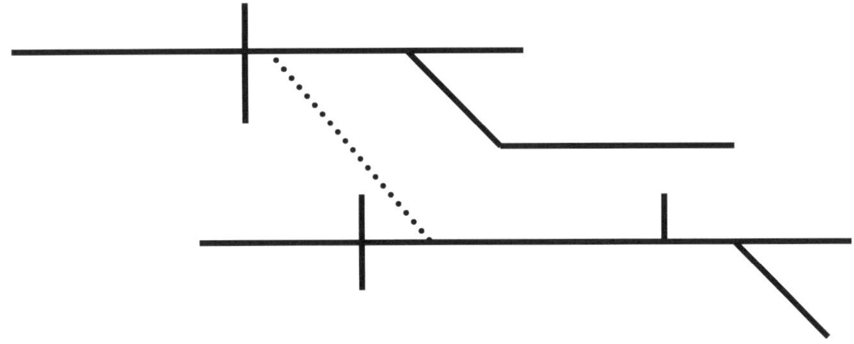

You cannot order from the children's menu if you are a teenager.

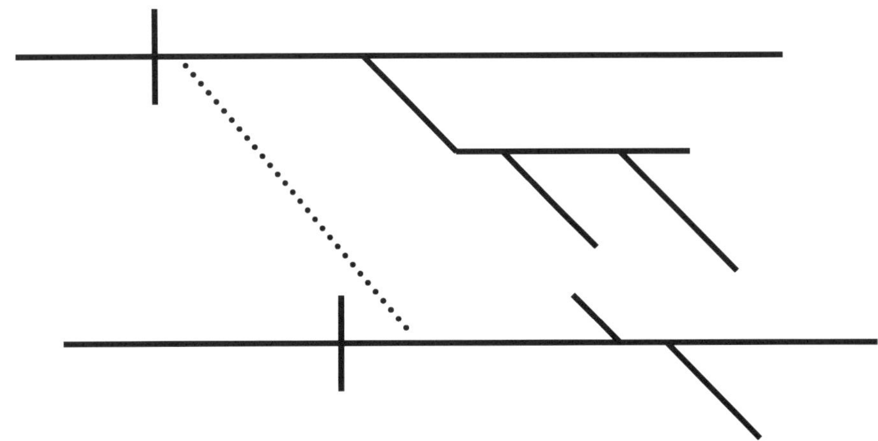

DIAGRAMMING

The complex sentence is diagrammed the same way whether the dependent clause comes first or not.

A comma is NOT needed if the complete sentence comes before the dependent clause.

5. Compound/Complex Sentence

WARNING! We now come to the Granddaddy of all sentences: the compound/complex sentence. It is a compound sentence because it consists of two complete sentences that could stand grammatically alone. It is a complex sentence because at least one of those complete sentences has a dependent clause with a subordinate conjunction. In fact, I could combine those two sentences above with a semi-colon and produce a magnificent example of a Compound/Complex sentence. In fact that is what I have done below.

It is a compound sentence because it consists of two complete sentences that could stand grammatically alone; it is complex because at least one of those complete sentences has a dependent clause with a subordinating conjunction.

This elegant sentence would be diagrammed like this:

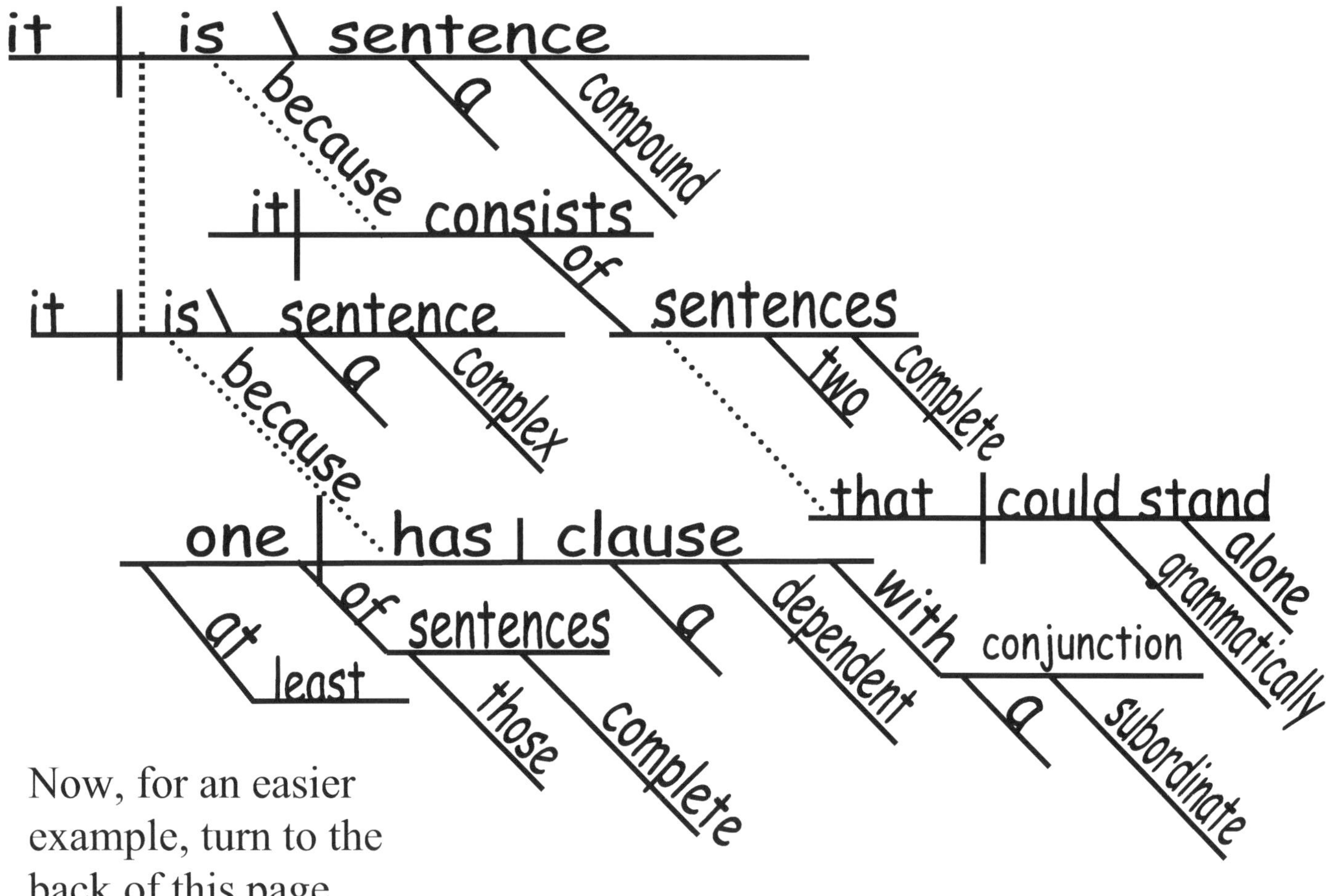

Now, for an easier example, turn to the back of this page.

I am a high school student, but my brother is a college student because he has graduated.

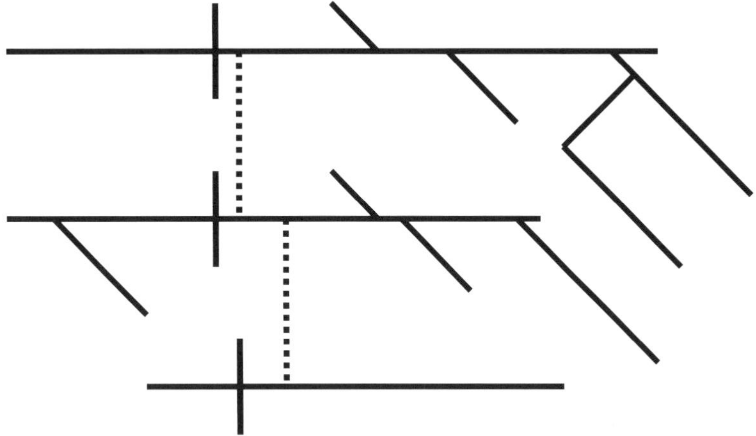

After the meeting ends, we will drive home; or we will go out to eat.

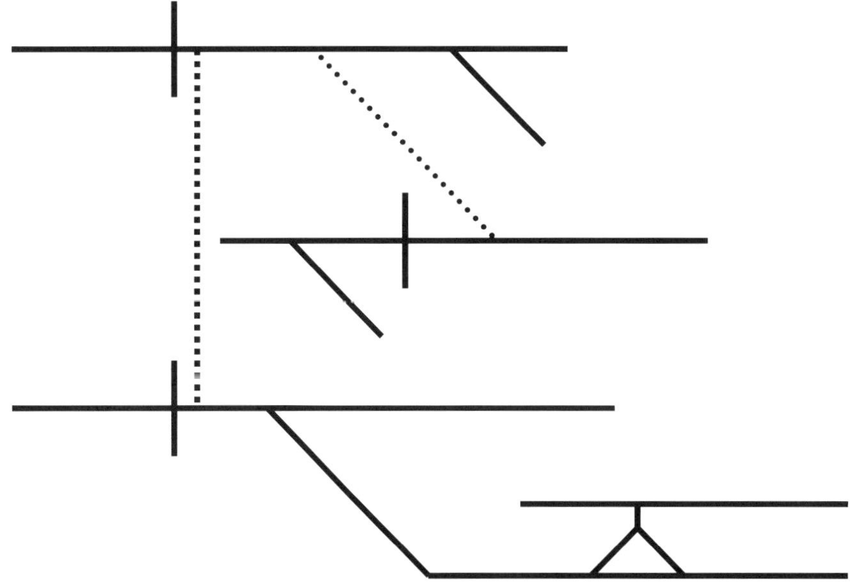

PUNCTUATION PEST

You're really going to think I'm pesky for this rule.

In most cases a compound sentence has either a comma conjunction **or** a semi-colon separating the two complete sentences.

In the last example, I used both a semi-colon and conjunction between the complete sentences. Actually, either can be correct and I've certainly seen writers use both. However, if you are faced with this question on a standardized test somewhere in the next few years, I would abide by this rule:

In a compound/complex sentence, a semi-colon and a conjunction may separate the two sentences if it clarifies the meaning of that sentence.

Finally, Mrs. Commafuss has been let out of the Grammar Slammer. She did ask me to remind you, one last time, to always remember that a comma is used when a dependent clause comes <u>before</u> the complete sentence and not when it comes after. She would remind you herself, except she is currently busy preparing her lecture on the ten usages of semi-colons. (Sounds like she may be heading to Punctuation Prison if she's not careful!)

EXPANDED TUTORAIL TOPIC LIST FOR GRAMMAR SLAMMER

1. Subject – Verb Sentences

The dog ate.

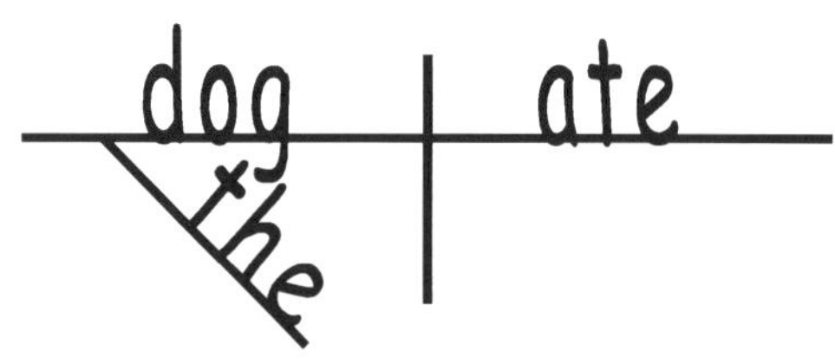

2. Subject – Verb – Direct Object

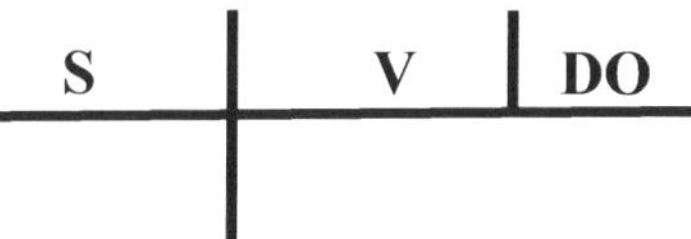

Our dog ate his bone.

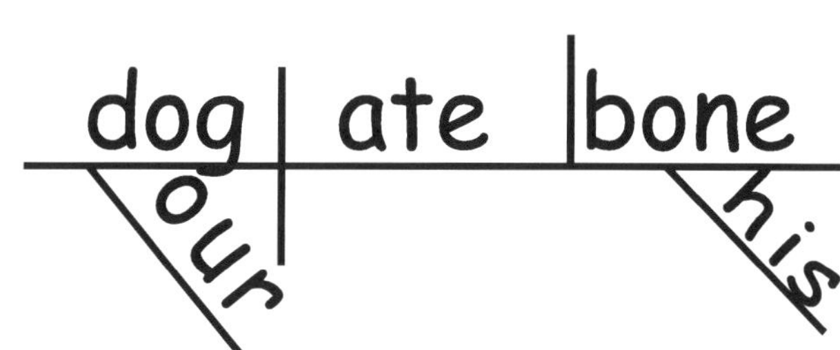

3. Subject – Verb - Indirect Object – Direct Object

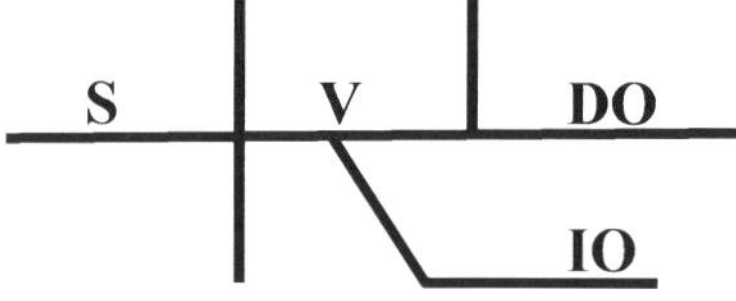

That dog gave the cat his toy.

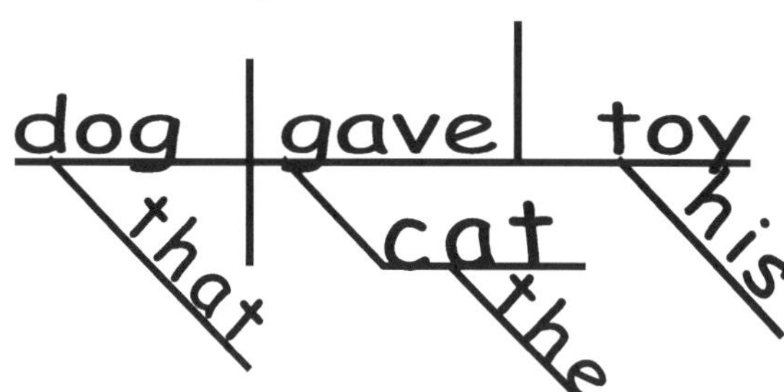

4. Subject – Linking Verb – Predicate Nominative

S | LV \ PN

This dog is my pet.

dog | is \ pet
this
my

5. Subject – Linking Verb - Adjective

S | LV / Adj

That puppy is cute.

puppy | is / cute
that

If you roll a six, roll again.

1. Proper Nouns
The subject (or any other noun) should name a specific person, organization, place, or era of history.

Amanda is a Collie.

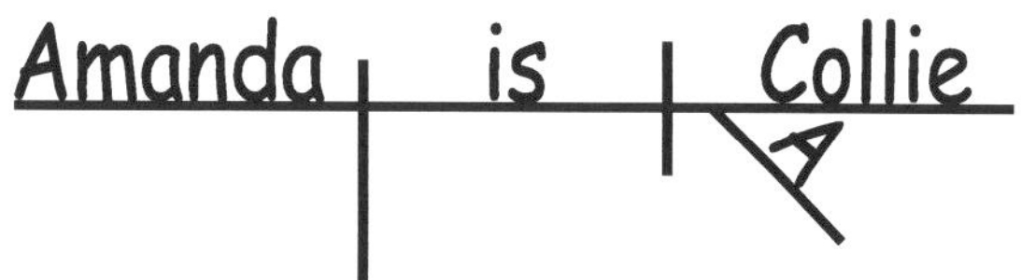

2. Compound Noun

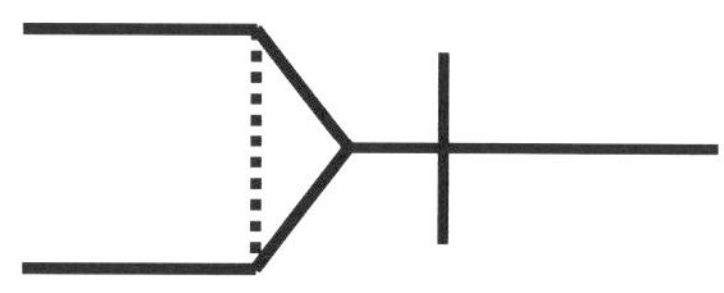

The dog and cat are sleeping

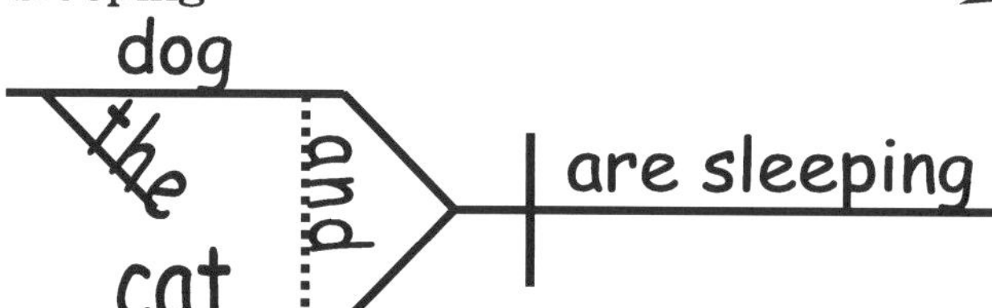

3. Personal Pronoun
Replace a noun with the correct personal pronoun.

	PERSON	NOMINATIVE CASE	OBJECTIVE CASE
S i n g	1st 2nd 3rd	I You He, She, It	Me You Him, Her, It
P l u r	1st 2nd 3rd	We You They	Us You Them

He is sleeping.

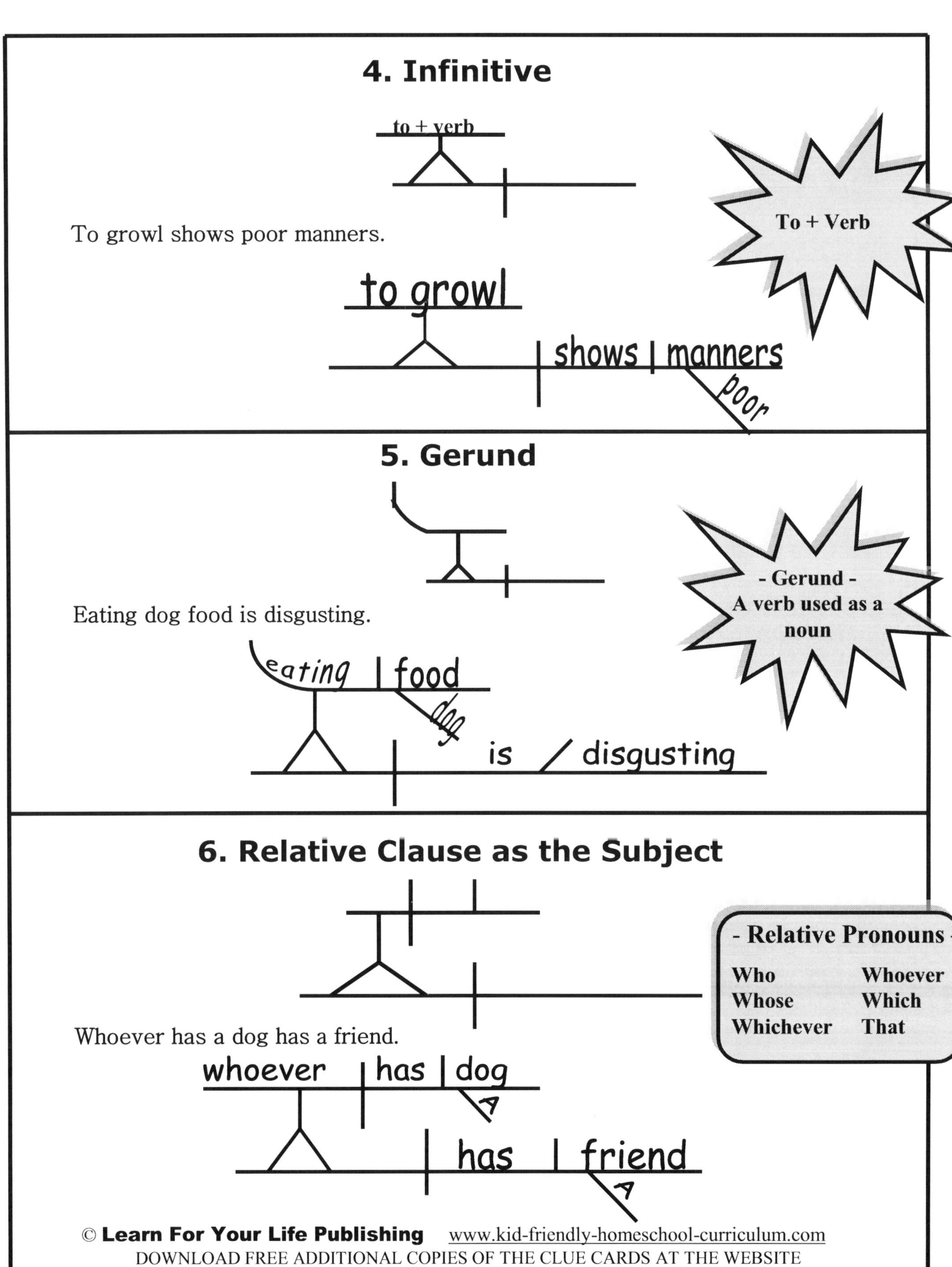

4. Infinitive
to + verb
To growl shows poor manners.
to growl
shows | manners
poor
To + Verb

5. Gerund
Eating dog food is disgusting.
eating | food
dog
is / disgusting
- Gerund -
A verb used as a noun

6. Relative Clause as the Subject
Whoever has a dog has a friend.
whoever | has | dog
has | friend
- Relative Pronouns -
Who   Whoever
Whose   Which
Whichever   That

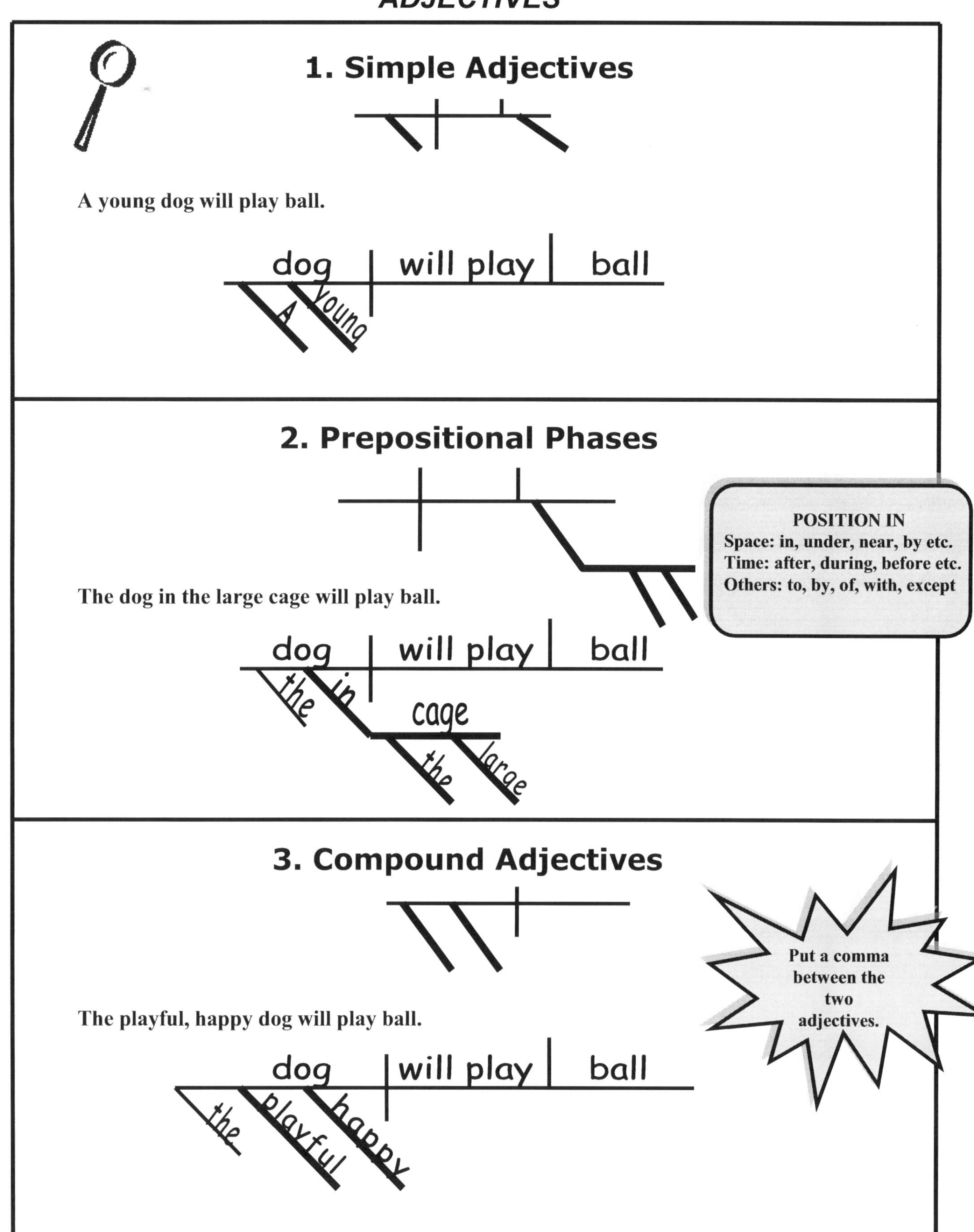
1. Simple Adjectives
A young dog will play ball.
dog | will play | ball
A young
2. Prepositional Phases
The dog in the large cage will play ball.
dog | will play | ball
the in
cage
the large
POSITION IN
Space: in, under, near, by etc.
Time: after, during, before etc.
Others: to, by, of, with, except
3. Compound Adjectives
The playful, happy dog will play ball.
dog | will play | ball
the playful happy
Put a comma between the two adjectives.

4. Participial Phrases

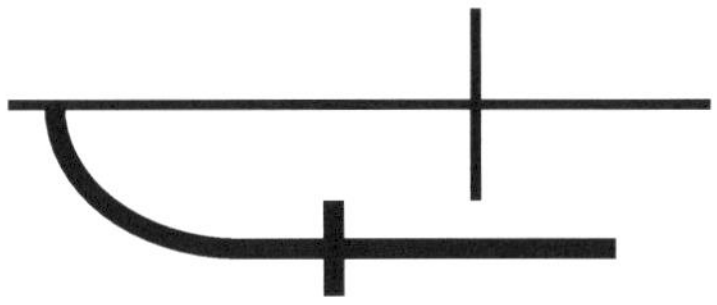

Participle = A verb form used as an adjective.

Seeing us, our dog will play ball.

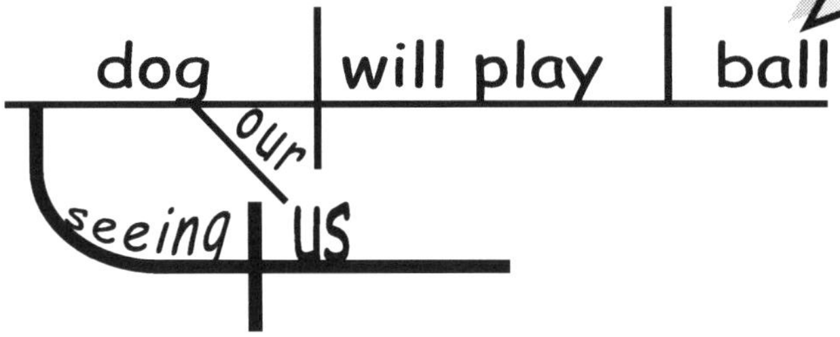

5. Relative Clause as an Adjective

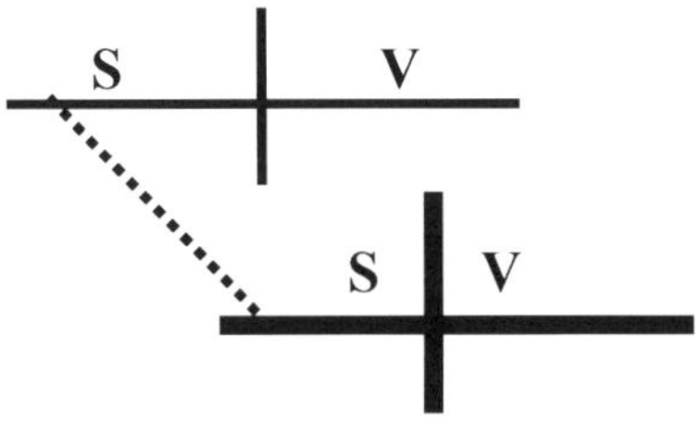

A relative clause begins with a relative pronoun.

Relative Pronouns
WHO, WHOM, WHICH, WHOSE, THAT

The dog who jumped the fence will play ball.

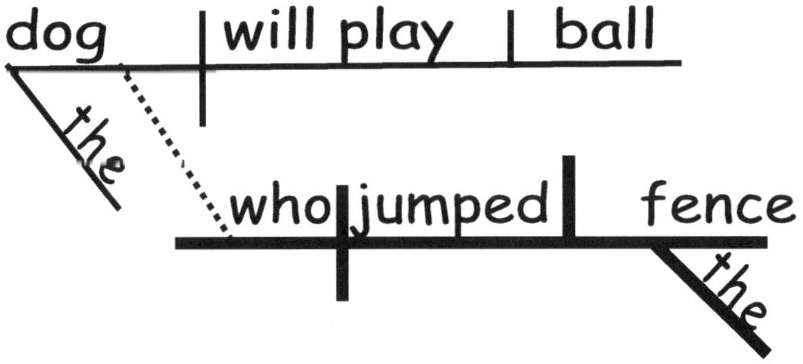

If you roll
a six,
roll again.

GRAMMAR SLAMMER
CLUE CARD D
VERB TENSES

1. Present Perfect - Progressive

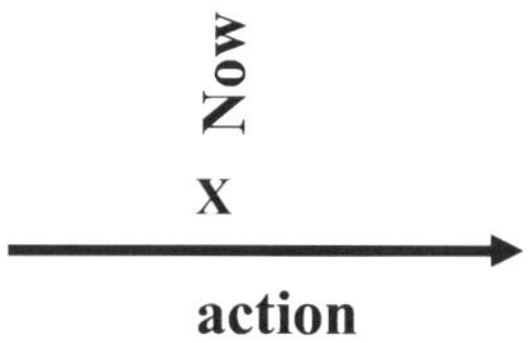

Rover has been growling at the man.

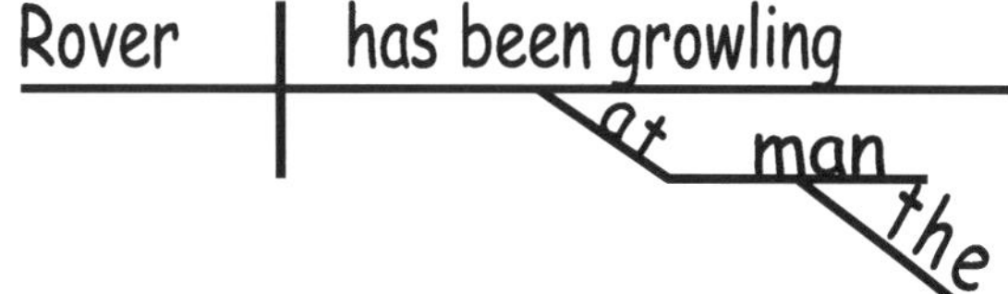

2. Past Perfect – Simple Action

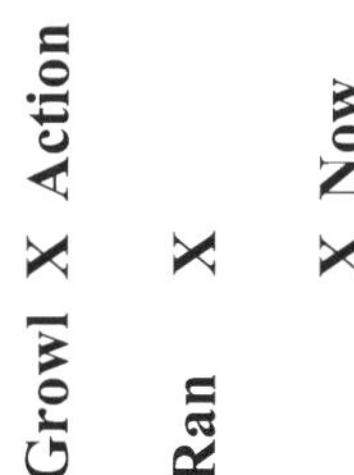

Rover had growled at the burglar who then ran away.

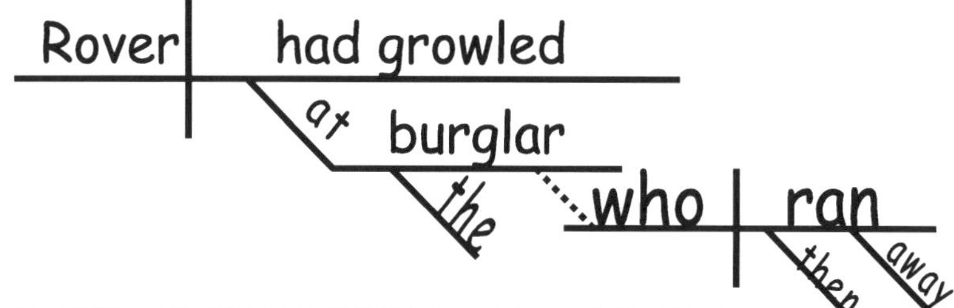

3. Past Perfect – Progressive Action

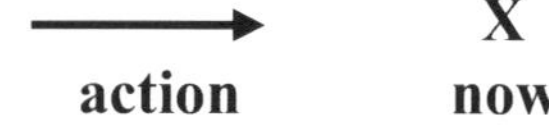

Rover had been growling at the burglar when the neighbors called the police.

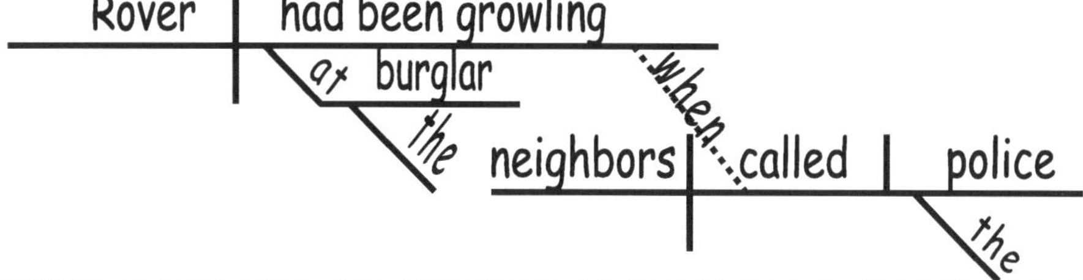

4. Future Perfect

Now
X

Future Action
X X

Rover will have been brushed
before the next dog show.

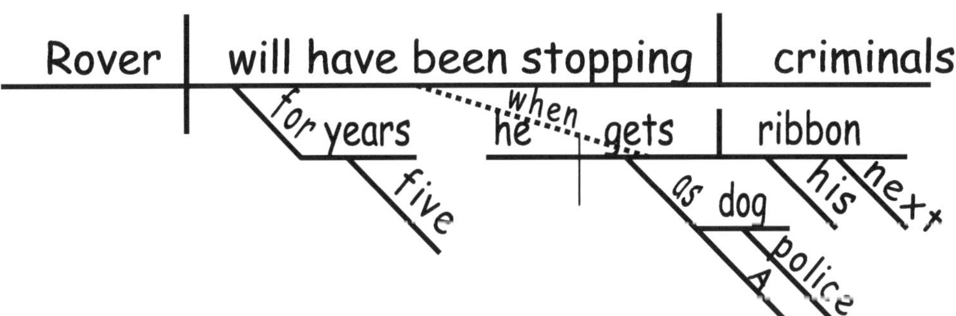

5. Future Perfect – Progressive Action

Now
X

Action
→

Rover will have been stopping criminals for five years when he gets his
next ribbon as a police dog.

6. Compound Verbs

Rover growled and barked at the convict.

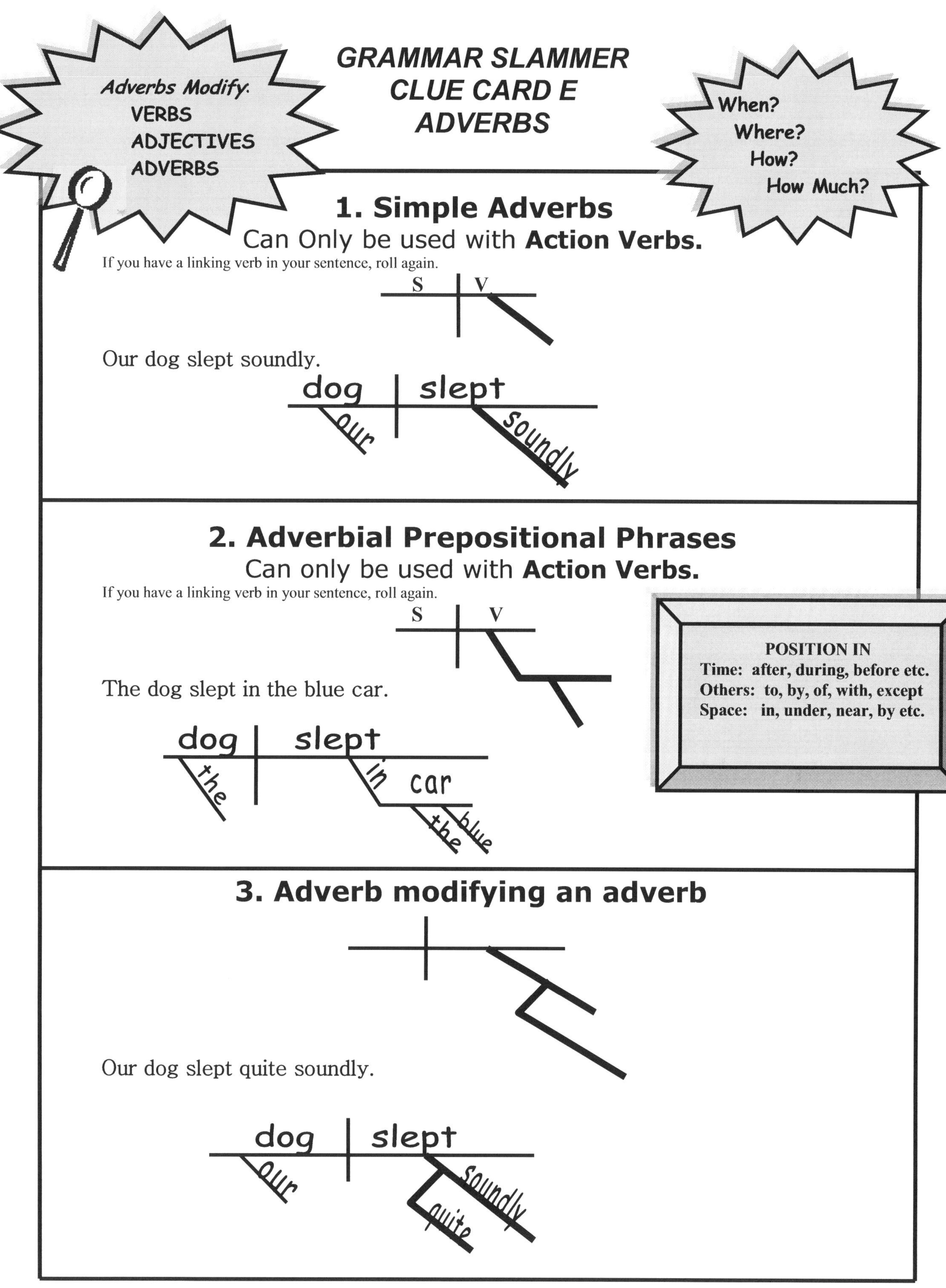

Adverbs Modify:
VERBS
ADJECTIVES
ADVERBS
GRAMMAR SLAMMER
CLUE CARD E
ADVERBS
When?
Where?
How?
How Much?

1. Simple Adverbs
Can Only be used with Action Verbs.
If you have a linking verb in your sentence, roll again.
S
V
Our dog slept soundly.
dog
slept
our
soundly

2. Adverbial Prepositional Phrases
Can only be used with Action Verbs.
If you have a linking verb in your sentence, roll again.
S
V
The dog slept in the blue car.
dog
slept
the
in
car
the
blue
POSITION IN
Time: after, during, before etc.
Others: to, by, of, with, except
Space: in, under, near, by etc.

3. Adverb modifying an adverb
Our dog slept quite soundly.
dog
slept
our
soundly
quite

4. Adverb modifying an adjective

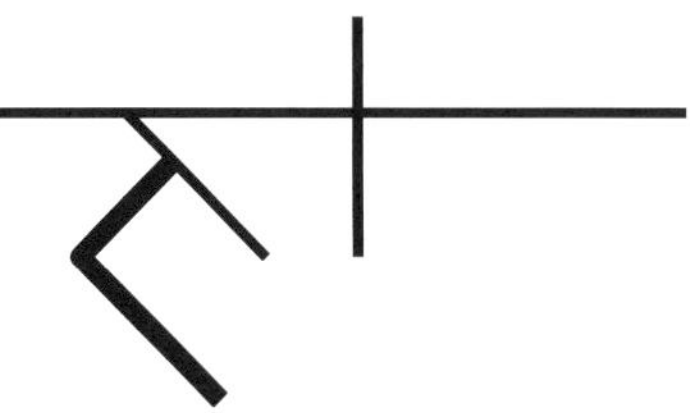

The extremely tired dog slept.

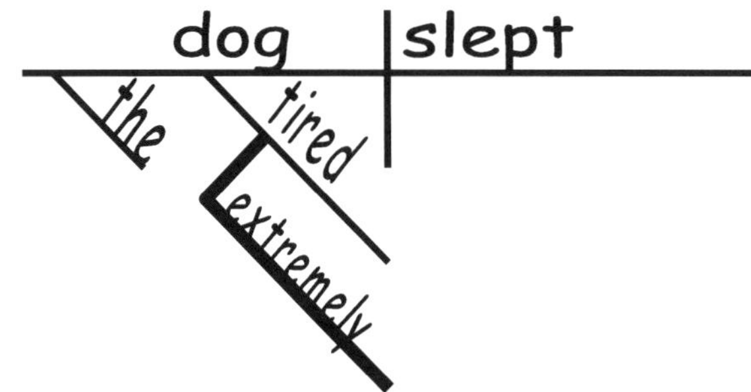

5. Complex Prepositional Phrases

His dog will sleep on the porch in back of the house.

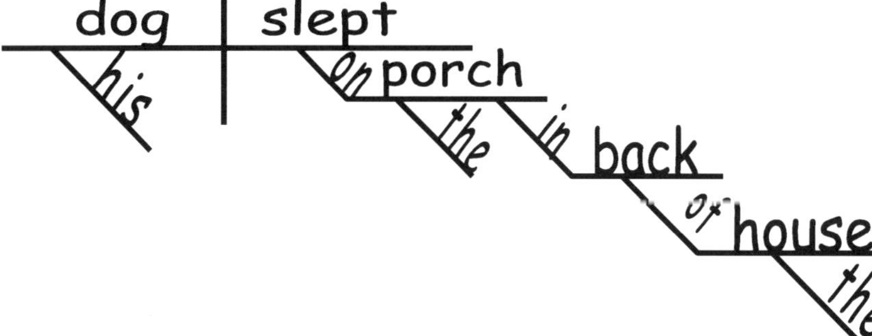

1. Interjections

Wow! That dog is large.

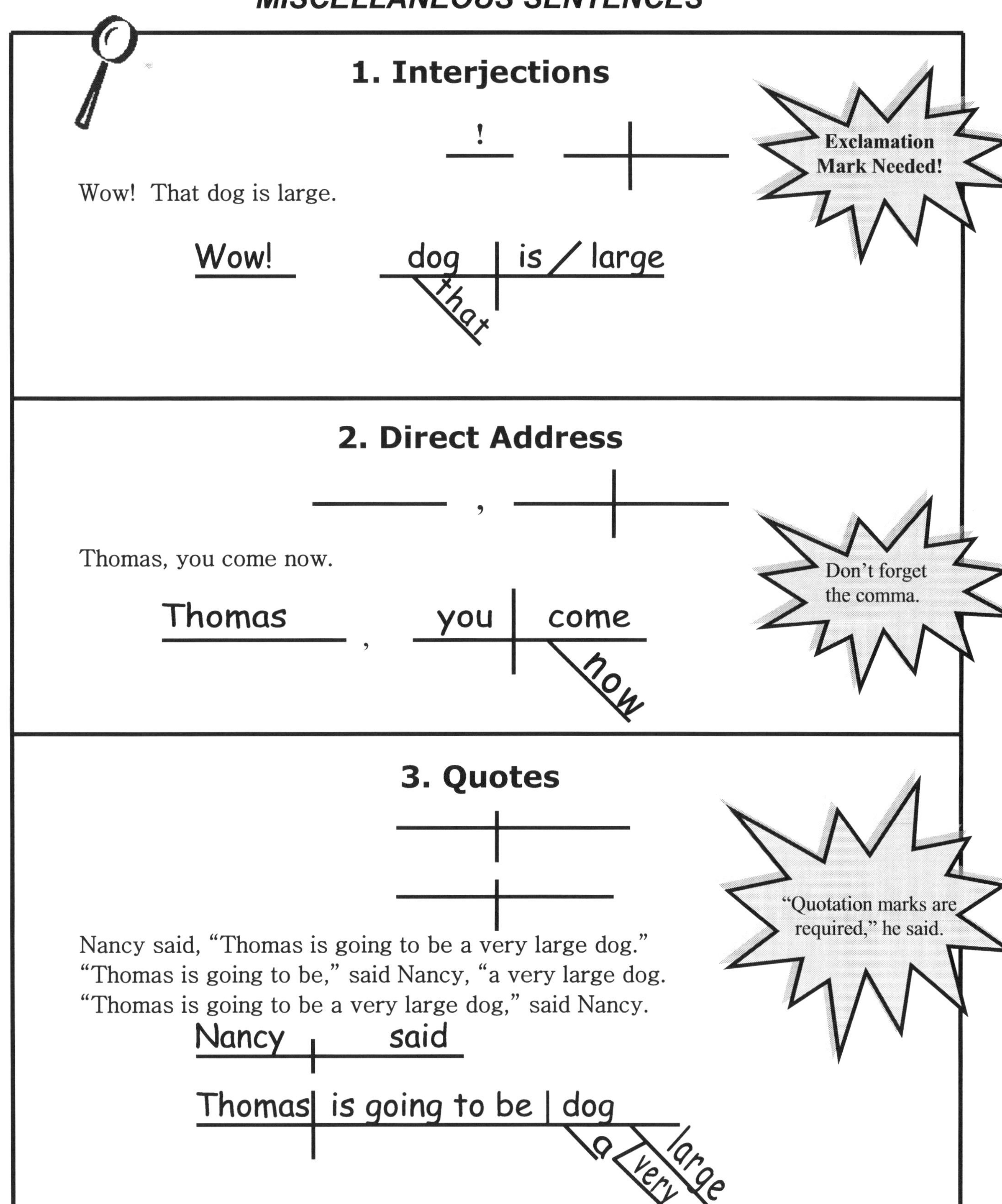

2. Direct Address

Thomas, you come now.

3. Quotes

Nancy said, "Thomas is going to be a very large dog."
"Thomas is going to be," said Nancy, "a very large dog.
"Thomas is going to be a very large dog," said Nancy.

4. Questions
Split the verb phrase.

VERB SPLIT

Thomas **will be** sixty-five pounds.

<u>Will</u> Thomas <u>be</u> sixty-five pounds?

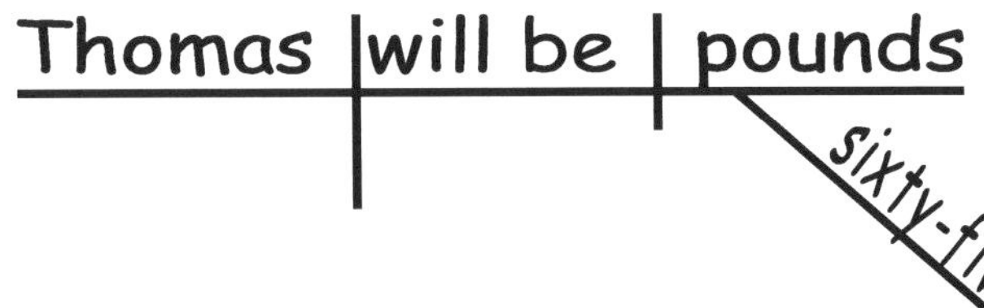

5. Appositive

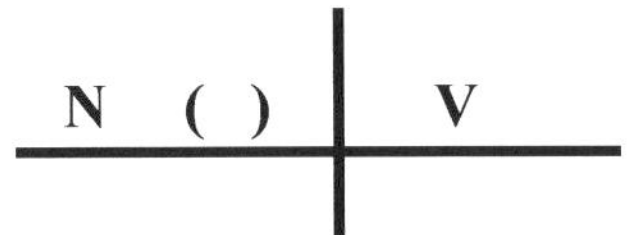

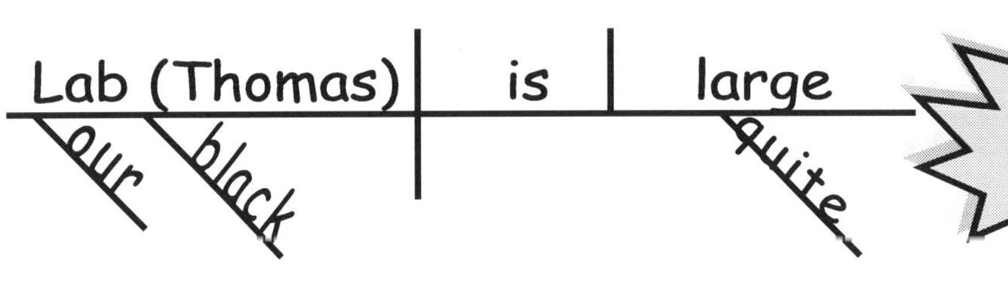

Our Black Lab, **Thomas,** is quite large.

Appositives
Restate the Noun

Commas
before and
after

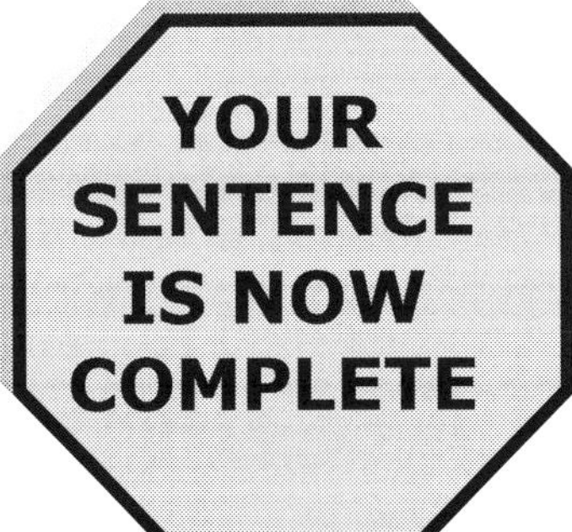

1. Compound with Comma – Conjunction

The German Shepherd is my dog, and the Scottish Terrier is my sister's dog.

2. Compound with semi-colon

The German Shepherd is my dog; the Scottish Terrier is my sister's dog.

3. Complex with comma

Because I like my dog, I take good care of her.

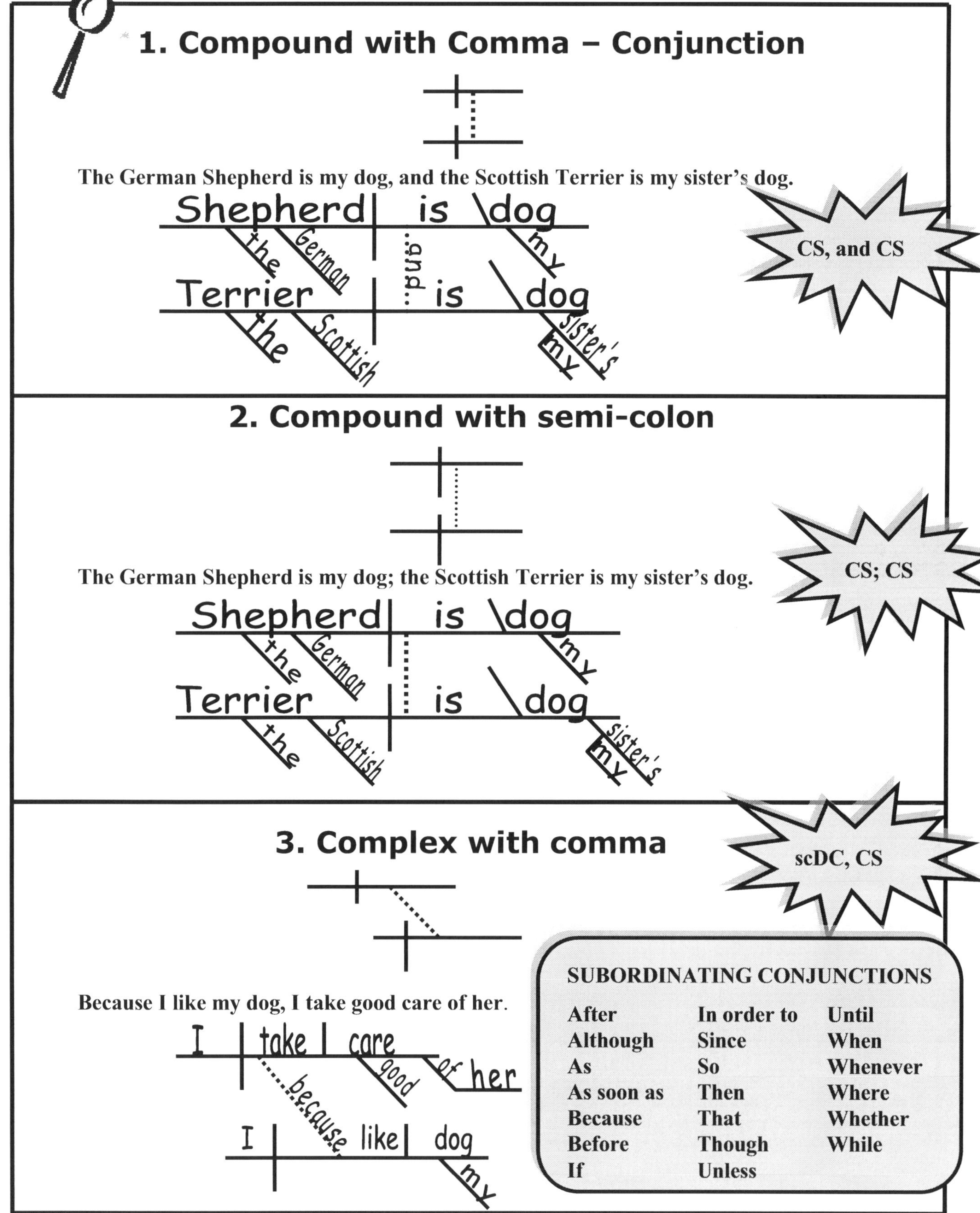

4. Complex without a comma

I take good care of my dog because I like her.

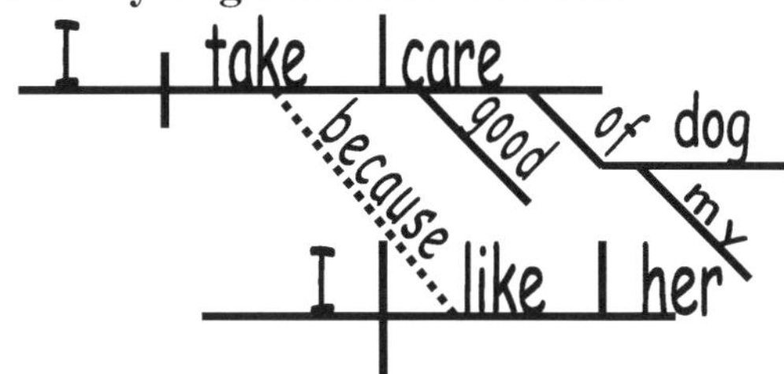

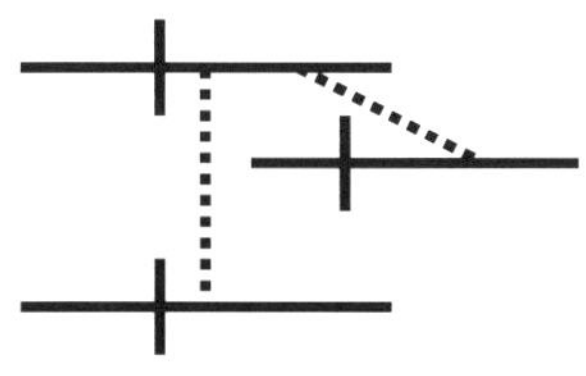

5. Compound/Complex Sentence

Our dog has won the state championship, and her puppy will compete in the next show because he is well trained.

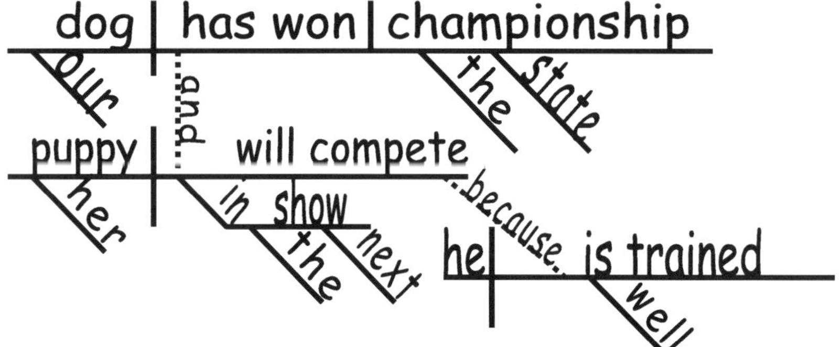

YOUR SENTENCE IS NOW COMPLETE

28344442R00064

Made in the USA
Charleston, SC
09 April 2014